In The Footsteps of My Fathers

A Family Way Through the Wars

James Bartlett

Printed in the United States of America

First Printing, 2020
Updated 2024
ISBN 978-1-7353222-3-0

Carentan Media Group
Fredericksburg, VA.
"Move, Shoot, and Communicate"
CarentanMedia@proton.me

For Dad.

Ride, shoot straight, and speak the truth.

Introduction

I had toyed with the idea of writing down all these wisps of family history for years. When the Covid pandemic hit, however, it took on a new urgency. If I died from this thing who would remember all these stories? Many of them had been entrusted only to me. I had just finished editing and doing the digital layout for MG Carol G. Childers book, "Cavalry Tales." I found myself back in the writing groove, so I retrieved this file I had started long ago.

They say that war runs in the family line. I believe this to be true. We are, after all, influenced by our parents, who were influenced by theirs, and so on. Culturally we feel this as well. Large conflicts, such as The Civil War, World War One, and World War Two, involve entire generations. They become part of the fabric of our collective conscious, our cultural identity, and our character. And finally, being a man draws one in as well. I have no doubt that buried in our primordial DNA is the natural instinct to hunt, fight, and defend. It is our ancient role in our tribes, regardless of geography or culture.

From an early age I felt this. Growing up in the age before digital entertainment and back to back super hero movies, I was exposed to the books on our shelves. I remember in particular a number of military history titles my father kept. I still have them. Most of these were richly illustrated with pictures. Fascination with these pictures turned into a lifetime of reading and eventually a youthful decision to "walk the walk." I have no doubt that these works helped put me on my own path to war.

Now mind you, this was not deliberate on the part of my father. His war experience in the Pacific was brutal and he held no notion of glory in any of it. He never lost an interest in it, however. Hence the books and his collecting various bits and pieces of memorabilia over the years. He didn't exactly encourage my interest in these things, and on a few occasions shut me down pretty hard over it. But still, as a child I would bring home this one book from the Memorial School library. A children's illustrated book on the Civil War. I would sit on his lap in the big blue chair and he would read it to me. I must have checked this book out at least four times. There was also a John Wayne movie called "The Horse Soldiers." It's one of the forgotten Wayne greats and it would come on Channel 8s "Sunday Great Show" twice a year. We watched that movie every time, every year. He would say, "Take a good look at that, you'll never see that in this day and age." I didn't have all the details, but I was keenly aware, early, that I had an ancestor who fought in that struggle.

By the time we got the cottage on Chebeague I was into an Age of Sail / Royal Navy phase. Summers were spent reading the Richard Bolitho series and playing Royal Marines vs. Colonials all over the island. I was also getting to the age where he would tell some stories from China and the Pacific.

And so it went, as I grew older the study of conflict became more structured and in depth until I eventually found myself downrange in various places. It helped me, I believe, to have such a broad range of knowledge. For starters it undoubtedly kept me alive on more than one occasion. Years of study had equipped me with a baseline knowledge of what to do, and not do. It made me far more cautious on a battlefield than other men my age. Early on I had appropriated his copy of "The ROTC Officers Manual for Cavalry, 1941 edition." Of particular interest was the scouting and patrolling chapters. I taught myself land navigation from that book, how to utilize cover, not to look over the top, how machine guns were employed, things like that. This was useful stuff to know when it came to places like Croatia or Bosnia.

I think I was better equipped emotionally as well. Even when things were bad, I could always draw on a larger perspective. That doesn't mean that I was unaffected or unhurt by things I witnessed over the years, I was. But at the end of the day I could say, "Well, it's not Antietam." I believe it has given me the ability to draw on a larger understanding when it comes to human conflict and I can put things in their proper compartments.

And we'll fill the vacant ranks
Of our brothers gone before
Shouting the battle cry of freedom...

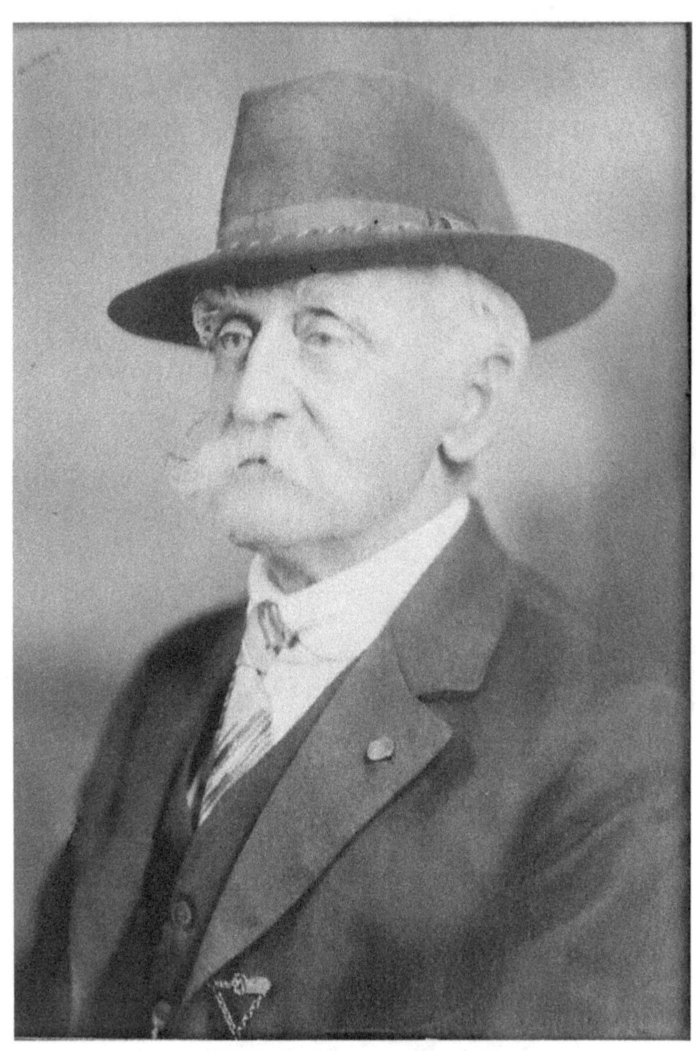

Pvt James Francis Bartlett
17th Maine Volunteer Infantry
Grand Army of the Republic

As he fought to make men holy, let us fight to make men free.

PVT James Francis Bartlett

17th Maine Volunteer Infantry

Virginia, 1862 - 1865

In many ways I feel closest to James Francis. He fought in a war whose cause I find to be noble, and one that has come to define a large part of my character. A war against a grave injustice for which a terrible price was paid to settle that account. It was fought by common folk from my native state and no doubt its memory echoed through our family consciousness over the generations. It certainly echoed through my father and it certainly echoes through me. They fought to make men free, as I myself did in a small way, in another country, 127 years later.

It was the beginning of industrialized war, and shocking in its destruction. It devastated an entire generation, and was quite literally an apocalypse for certain parts of the country. There had never been anything like it. No generation had ever been flung so far from home for so long and felled in such great numbers. It touched every home, no matter how remote. It claimed the lives of young men from Deer Island, Maine to Glorieta Pass, New Mexico to the coast of France.

It was the last major war where a regimental flag was carried onto an active battlefield. At least they had that. It ultimately defined us as a single, united country.

James was born August 18th, 1847. He was the son of Alexander Paine Bartlett, a joiner by trade in Portland, and Clarissa Jackson Bartlett. He was the youngest of four children by Clarissa and Alexander; Sarah, Charles and brother George who died before James was born, aged two. In 1850 Clarissa died, when James was three. His father remarried in December 1852 to Hannah Libby, who would have naturally assumed the role of his mother. Alexander and Hannah had another George and a daughter Clara, who died in 1859 at age three. James would have been twelve and this doubtless was a traumatic event for the whole family. The next spring, March of 1860, he would lose his father as well.

Larger trauma was in the offing, however, as the country careened towards war with the election of Lincoln in in November of 1860. The following spring Union and Confederate armies collided near Manassas Virginia and it started to dawn on people that this war would not be a quick and easy affair. A little over a year later, in August of 1862, James would be signing enlistment papers as a musician (drummer) in B Company, 17th Maine Volunteer Infantry. He had just turned fifteen years old.

Strangely, however, the roster of Captain George Martin, commanding B Co, lists his age as 18. Either he lied or they pencil whipped it so he could draw full pay, which was not uncommon. Either way, James and the 17th Maine were shortly on their way to the war in Virginia.

The regiment would find itself engaged many times over during its time there and suffered the highest battle casualties of any Maine Regiment during the war, mostly on a single day at Gettysburg in the Wheatfield. Repeated bloodlettings bumped those numbers, especially when Grant crossed the Rapidan in May of 1864, headed towards Lee and Richmond, never to turn back.

The journey from being a child in Maine to his return as a veteran of that great war started in the Army camps around Cape Elizabeth and Washington DC, where the regiment fell in for capitol defense duty through September and into October of 1862. His life would have been one of drill, drill and more drill, followed by posting of the guards, eating, sleeping, and more drill. He would have had the added duty of learning and memorizing a host of different drum beats used in those days to relay orders over the sound of battle. He may also have had some tutelage from the regimental surgeon, as musicians not engaged in relaying orders were detailed as helpers for the wounded.

The regiment moved through Virginia, to Gettysburg, back to Virginia, and ultimately returned to Washington following the surrender of Lee at Appomattox Courthouse in April of 1865. During that time the 17th was present at every major engagement the Army of the Potomac fought, and more than a few minor ones.

There is an excellent book that details the actions of the 17th Maine, so I will not write their entire history here. It is; [The Red Diamond Regiment: The 17th Maine Infantry 1862 – 1865, by William B. Jordan.] Specific information regarding him in the books is lacking. There is no mention in dispatches, no great deeds noted. He just did whatever job was assigned. He experienced that war as an average, private soldier in the Army of the Potomac, right along with tens of thousands of others whose names and deeds live only in the line items of the duty rosters. "Hard Tack and Coffee: The Unwritten Story of Army Life," is an excellent memoir by John D. Billings that covers aspects of army life in detail.

A few wisps of memory made it down through the years, from my own father. He was a drummer, not very tall. Eventually, after the losses at Wilderness, they told him to lose the drum and get a Springfield, which he carried through the end of that war. It was almost as tall as he was. He was slightly wounded in the hand at Petersburg by a rebel sharpshooter. Nothing that required the attention of a field hospital necessarily, but it certainly must have gotten everyone's attention. Richard "Dick" Bartlett remembered playing with his kepi when he and dad were children. In those days of the late 20s and 30s, James was an old, gray veteran before passing in 1934. He was a member in good standing of the GAR (The Grand Army of the Republic, a veterans organization) and lived long enough to see great grandchildren.

I will add some reflections and events of my own. Some of it may sound a little "Whoo-hooey" but bear with it. It happened, things were revealed, as sometimes happens to me.

I was visiting Gettysburg some years ago, 2016-ish if recall. I was down in the Wheatfield. I went to the wall where they made a stand in what was a really bad position that the entire corps had been led into by the inexplicable actions of Gen. Dan Sickles (hotly debated to this day). I pushed past the wall into the woods where the Confederates had made their repeated attempts to dislodge the stubborn Mainers. It was a hot section of woods, a lot of guys got killed there.

Now, I am no fan of the Confederacy or their cause. The spirits that still hold those woods know this, they have to, it radiates from me. So I'm walking through and the first branch slaps me across the face. OK, I somehow missed a bent branch, big deal. I keep walking deeper in. BAM! Another one, this time hard. Sorry, but I've been walking through woods my whole life, I don't go bending back branches that then strike back so hard they leave a welt and knock my glasses off. That's when I felt them, very present, very angry. "These are our woods, Yankee, you git out!" OK, OK, I get it, no problem. I start back towards the wall. When I was about ten feet away from it, another reb slid up and whispered, "This is as far as we got. I'll give it to 'em, they fought like hell, they didn't want to come up off that wall."

So you can imagine the kind of struggle that was taking place there. Vicious. Two desperate groups of men trying to kill each other at close range with large bore, black powder muskets. One side is stuck in an untenable spot but behind some solid cover. They have to hang there, if they break, they're toast. And here comes another group, if they don't break through and win this fight they too are finished. North of the river in front of a larger army, very far from home. It was the makings of a savage struggled and the Mainers of the 17th and George Anderson's Georgia brigade were stuck right in the middle of it. At one point they fell back, but quickly retook the wall and held it with bayonets. Seven color bearers were shot down by the end of the day. 132 men were killed, wounded, or missing out of a scant 351 who went in.

So I wander away from the wall and towards the rear, where there was a battery of guns set up on a rise behind them a hundred yards or so away. I'm not moving in any direction with purpose, just meandering. I get halfway up the hill and I'm struck like a jolt, sudden, locked to the spot I'm on. A voice, a Maine voice, not from anywhere but everywhere, inside me. "You've seen a thing or two son, but you ain't seen nothing like this." I turn, I see the field behind me. Not with my eyes, but as if in memory, as if he shock loaded them into my head.

It's like I'm suddenly wearing someone else's Go-Pro.

A writing carpet of blue. Covered. The dead and dying intermingled. It is overwhelming. I turn back, there's a man on the ground, someone turns him over. His head is cleaved open from above his right eyebrow to his left cheek, wide open, a startled look on his face. "He were a friend of mine," the voice intoned. It was a shell burst, case shot, air bursting. He was bringing him to the rear, it knocked them both down. Only one of them got up. It's hitting me like a punch in the guts.

The scene carries on, up the hill, running. He's running and he keeps running, past the guns and into the limbers in their rear. He falls, hands and knees. A man is running past, shot bag, bringing another round to the guns, dirty, dark brown hair, bowel cut. He stops, grabs the boy's shoulder, firmly, like an older brother would. "C'mon son, pull yourself together." The boy looks up. "You can do it, c'mon now." The boy nodded. Got to his feet, turned, and went back in. He was 15 ½ yrs old.

I was pretty emotional by this point, but he said, "We're all OK. We're OK now. We're glad you think on us now and again. But you've got things to do so you run on now. You're gonna be ok, you're a good man so stop worrying, everything will work out. But you go on now."

The encounter left me shaken for a week.

The muster rolls and after action report I recently found for that engagement list PVT James F. Bartlett (Musician) as being on "Detached Service," detailed to tend wounded that day. I'm pretty sure that that was the day when war stopped being a grand, boys adventure. Up until then, it kinda had been. The 17th Maine had been present at every major engagement, and Chancellorsville had definitely been an affair, with 113 casualties. But they'd never been in a spot like this where it had gone full blown battle insanity at close range with bayonets. It was the day that it all got very, very real.

Worse would follow at Wilderness, where they tangled with Longstreet's Corps and were then caught up in the forest fire that broke out, losing 183 total. From there it was a steady bloodletting, in packets of a few dozen or more, here and there, all the way to the end. The Bloody Angle at Spotsylvania; 54. Cold Harbor; 23. Petersburg; 84 total in various trench battles from June of '64 to March of '65, including a particularly ugly affair during the long march to raid the Weldon Railroad. Upon returning they found that some of their stragglers and sick who had been left behind had been murdered by Southern villagers. They torched the place in revenge. That was in December of '64, so he would have been just over 17 years old.

On another occasion he came to me again, as I walked the battlefield where the 17th had pushed on after the main engagement at Sailors Creek. This had been a decisive Union victory during the pursuit of Lee after he abandoned the Petersburg lines and fled towards Appomattox. The final crescendo happened at the double bridge on Little Sailors Creek below Locketts Farm (Dentonville) where they had advanced into a big fight around the bogged down wagon trains of what was left of Gen. John B. Gordon's II Corps. As night fell and the battered Confederates withdrew, the troops began to rummage and loot the wagons.

Inside there were supplies and officers baggage of every description. The boys were mightily pleased. They were winning, had suffered few casualties, and had now scored a big pile of loot. Spirits were high. At one point he pried open a small trunk, obviously an officers, finding a locket amongst the items. It was silver and held a picture of a young woman with dark, prim hair. A sudden sadness overcame him and he put it back. "I couldn't bring myself to take it. I wondered now and again, over the years, whatever became of that man."

Three days later Lee surrendered to Grant and the war was over.

Returning home, the 17th was treated to a grand welcome in Portland. The Mayor and citizens of note threw them a picnic but made the mistake of setting the tables with hard tack and salt pork, apparently thinking this would be a nice reminiscence. The soldiers nearly rioted, turning the tables over and crushing the vile stuff into the dirt before storming away to the nearest pub. Like many other veterans he joined the G.A.R. (Grand Army of the Republic) and was likely active in their endeavors during the post war years.

On August 5th, 1868 he married Clara Susan Huston of Falmouth, (who died in 1911) in Portland. Together they had eight children, including Frank Randle Bartlett, my grandfather's father.

James went on to become an Electrician with Central Maine Power Co, raised his family, and died on the 19th of September 1934, in Topsham, ME. Dad would have been 9 years old.

Strange coincidence

Pvt Charles Milliken served as a hospital orderly to the surgeon of the 17th Maine. As the musicians were detailed as stretcher bearers he undoubtedly came into close contact with Pvt. Bartlett.

Fast forward 90 years and Bartlett's Great-grandson, my father William, married Milliken's great-granddaughter, Elizabeth, my stepmother.

Didn't see that one coming in the research.

17th Maine Volunteers List of Organizational Assignments

* 3rd Brigade, 1st Division, 3rd Army Corps, through March, 1864.

* 2nd Brigade, 3rd Division, 2nd Army Corps, to June, 1864.
(Following transfer to 2nd Corps, the Regiment petitioned to retain the Red Diamond shaped corps insignia they wore while with 3rd Corps. They were allowed to keep it and wear on their uniform, instead of the cap, to avoid confusion. Thusly they became known as "The Red Diamond Regiment")

* 1st Brigade, 3rd Division, 2nd Corps, to March, 1865.

* 2nd Brigade, 3rd Division, 2nd Corps, to June, 1865.

Service / Campaigns

They departed Portland and Cape Elizabeth on August 21st, 1862 and they show up on the organization for the defenses of the capitol on October 7, 1862.

Battle of Fredericksburg December 12-15. 1862
(Engaged east of Slaughter Pen Farm, Birney's Brigade)
"Mud March" January 20-24, 1863.

Chancellorsville Campaign April 27-May 6. 1862
Battle of Chancellorsville May 1-5. 113 Killed, wounded, missing.

Gettysburg Campaign June 13-July 24. 1863
Battle of Gettysburg July 1-3. 132 killed, wounded, missing.
Pursuit of Lee July 5-24.
Wapping Heights July 23.

Bristoe Campaign October 9-22. 1863
Auburn and Bristoe October 14.
Advance to line of the Rappahannock November 7-8.
Kelly's Ford November 7.

Mine Run Campaign November 26-December 2. 1863-4
Payne's Farm November 27.
Mine Run November 28-30.
Demonstration on the Rapidan February 6-7, 1864.

Grants Overland Campaign 1864

Battles of the Wilderness May 5-7.
Laurel Hill May 8.

Spotsylvania May 8-12.
Po River May 10.

Spotsylvania C. H. May 12-21.
"Bloody Angle," Assault on the Salient, May 12.
Harris Farm, Fredericksburg Road, May 19.

North Anna May 23-26.
Line of the Pamunkey May 26-28.
Totopotomoy May 28-31.

Cold Harbor June 1-12.

Siege of Petersburg June 16, 1864 –March 28th, 1865.
Siege of Petersburg June 16, 1864, to April 2, 1865.
Jerusalem Plank Road June 22-23, 1864.
Deep Bottom, north of the James, July 27-28.
Mine Explosion, Petersburg, July 30.
Demonstration north of the James August 13-20.
Strawberry Plains August 14-18.
Ream's Station August 25.

Poplar Springs Church September 29-October 2.
Boydton Plank Road, Hatcher's Run, October 27-28.
Raid on Weldon Railroad December 7-11.
Dabney's Mills February 5-7, 1865.

The Final Campaign, 1965

Appomattox Campaign March 28-April 9.
South Side Railroad March 29.
Boydton Road and White Oak Ridge March 30-31.
Fall of Petersburg April 2.
Jettersville April 5.
Sailor's Creek / Locketts Farm April 6.
High Bridge April 6-7.
Farmville April 7.

Appomattox C. H. April 9.
Surrender of Lee and his army. At Burkesville April 11-May 1.

March to Washington, D. C., May 1-15.
Grand Review May 23.
Mustered out at Bailey's Cross Roads June 4, 1865.
Recruits transferred to 1st Maine Heavy Artillery. Veterans discharged at Portland, Me., June 10, 1865.

Regiment lost during service 12 Officers and 195 Enlisted men killed and mortally wounded and 4 Officers and 159 Enlisted men by disease. Total 370. (One of the highest overall losses for a Maine Regiment)

Pvt William Casto

Killed in Action

Jackson, MS. July 11th, 1863

On my mothers side of the family I grew up with stories of my great-grandfather. His patriotism was notable, as was his business acumen, having founded Dodge Motors with his cousin Horace. When WW1 came, there was no question that John Dodge would do whatever he could to support the effort, once America entered the war. And he did, taking on a major role in the mass production of the trench busting 155mm howitzer that the French were unable to produce in numbers.

When approached by the government to see if something could be done, he immediately agreed, with one condition; no govt inspectors looking over his shoulder. Horace would redesign the troublesome recoil mechanism and a machine to automate the process, while John would build the factory. They would do this for nearly cost. The govt agreed and soon this powerful system was moving to France in numbers.

While patriotism was not in short supply during that time, an established industrialist doing the job for no to little profit was not. I wondered where he came by that notion. Pretty sure it was his mother, Maria Casto. You see, she had a baby brother named William. She was 10 when he was born, and as was the way in those times, she very much helped raise him.

Like many others from Nile's Michigan, he mustered into E Company, 2nd Michigan Infantry in the spring of 1861 during Lincoln's first call for troops. It was likely that he was one of the original members of the state militia unit known as the "Niles Company." In short order the militia units were rostered as 3yr regiments and soon departed Ft. Wayne for the east in May of 1861. William would have been 20 years old.

Arriving at Washington soon after they were engaged in the general skirmishing that took place in the environs of Northern Virginia. The First Battle of Bull Run teed off not long after and while not engaged the 2nd wound up covering the retreat of the army after the stinging rout that occurred there. Welcome to the war, kid.

While that early engagement must have been exciting, a real blooding was to come when Gen. McClellan led his reformed and thoroughly drilled army into the Peninsula Campaign, culminating in the Seven Days battles outside Richmond. Starting at Williamsburg, the regiment found itself bloodied again and again. The war was no longer a boys adventure. William and his comrades settled in for a long haul.

Through 1862 and the winter of 1863 they served through the generally miserable conditions around Fredericksburg, and for a time were billeted next to the 17th Maine (James Franklin Bartlett, Greatt-grandfather on my father's side) while assigned to 3rd Brigade of the 1st Division under Birney. They may have even played baseball against each other.

In March of 1863, William and his comrades were transferred to the Western theater of war under General Grant. By June they were headed to his siege outside Vicksburg, Mississippi. After a short time outside the city, they were detailed to general Sherman who was establishing exterior lines to the east in response to a Confederate relief force under Confederate Gen. Johnson. William's time was getting short.

Johnson was not going to arrive in time and on July 4th Vicksburg finally surrendered. Johnson fell back to Jackson, pursued by Sherman. Arriving on the north side of town someone decided to "have a go" at the Confederate fortifications, sending in the 2nd and two other regiments. Rushing towards a position known as "The cotton bale battery" the 2nd came under a withering fire, but pushed forward despite. Soon, however, the other two units on either flank gave way and retreated, compelling the 2nd to do the same.

William Casto, however, was not among them when they finally made it out of range. Somewhere in the confusion he had been killed outright, his body left on the field. He was 22yrs old.

The historical marker that marks the spot reads; "Though heavily outnumbered, the Michiganders fought to within 200 yards of the fortified ridge before Col. William Humphrey gave the order to retire." Another account wrote of it as a "gallant dash, finest charge you ever saw." Along with William, 12 others lay dead in the dirt. Some days later Johnson retired in good order and Sherman occupied the town.

The bodies of the dead Michigan boys were policed up and buried on the grounds of the insane asylum north of town. For his sacrifice his name was accorded one line in the regimental roster, the discharge column notated as "Killed, Jackson MS July 11th 1863." It appears nowhere else, in neither official reports or the diaries of survivors.

Sometime later, maybe weeks or months later, his older sister, the girl who helped raise him, watched him grow to manhood, received a letter. Your baby brother is dead.

That's what hits me the hardest, as I read the journals, the regimental histories, the official reports. Not one mention of his name. Everyone just kept on going. One minute this 22yr old kid was dashing with his friends across that contested field, the next he's lying there with the life smashed out of him. No one recorded a single detail. Did he die instantly? Did he lose a leg and bleed out? Gut shot? Nobody noticed. And then they just left him in a hasty grave and marched away.

I've seen it myself time and again. Done it myself. But for some reason this one haunts me. I never knew him, not even close, but it bothers me. I have no doubt the anguish his sister felt, my Great-great-grandmother, echoed across the ages. That's something you just don't get over. Born only 2 years later, my grandfather Dodge no doubt became aware of the meaning of nation and what it took to preserve it. When a war effort called, he didn't hesitate.

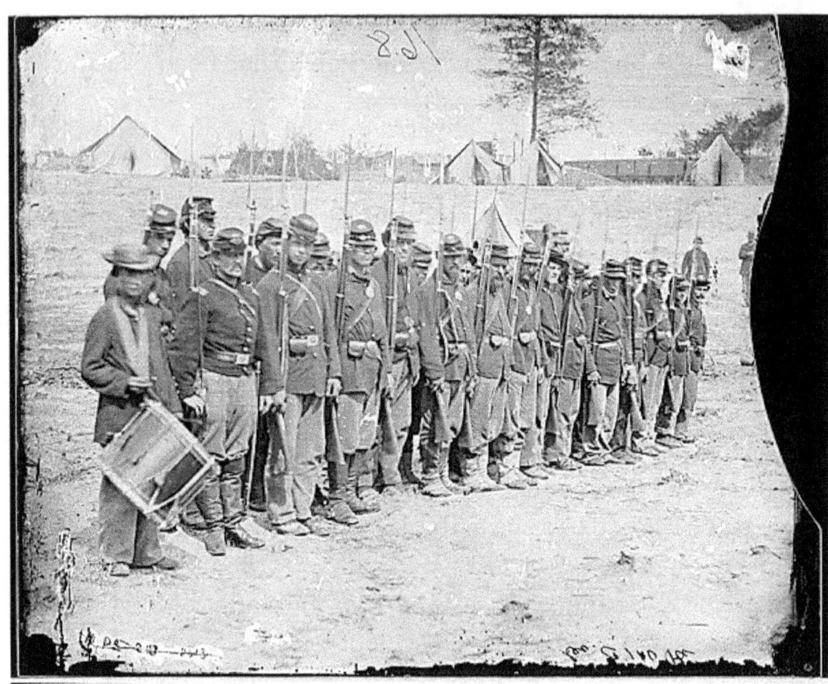

Typical company of Union infantry, drawn up in firing line with their drummer. During the war 72,945 Mainers served, 7,322 of whom were killed. It was a transformational experience for an entire generation.

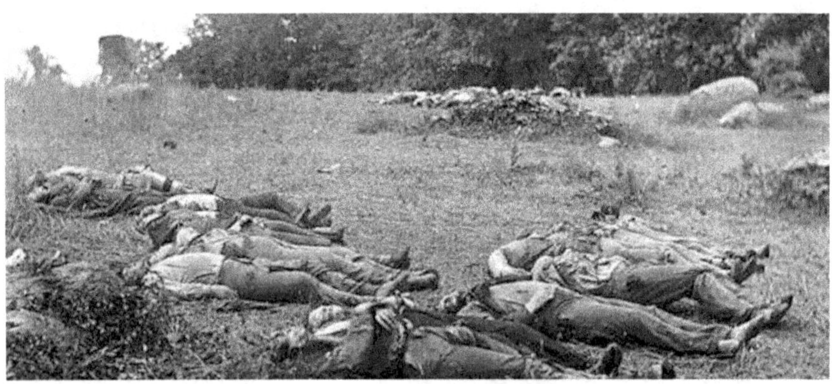

"...that from these honored dead we take increased devotion to that cause for which they gave the last full measure of devotion—that we here highly resolve that these dead shall not have died in vain—that this nation, under God, shall have a new birth of freedom." A. Lincoln.

Aftermath in the Wheatfield, Gettysburg, July, 1863. The 17th Maine went onto the field with 351 men and came off with little more than 200.

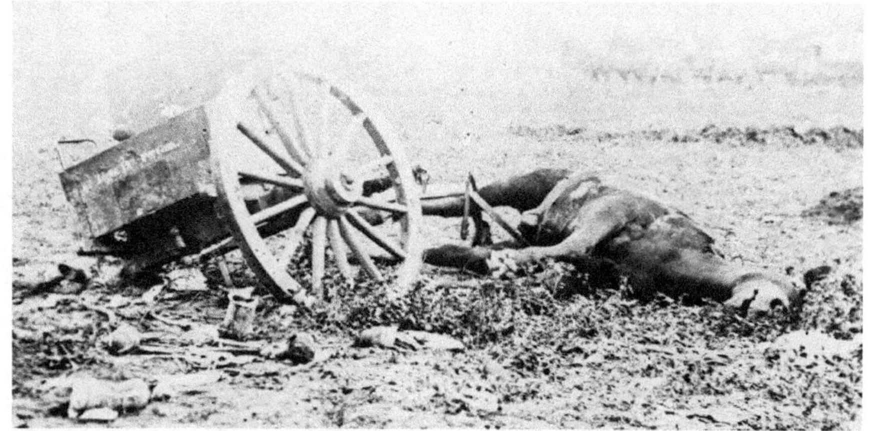

Slaughter of the innocents. The Union Army lost over 13,000 horses and mules at Gettysburg and the pursuit of Lee to Virginia. For years afterward soldiers suffered from a form of post traumatic depression known as "Soldiers Heart." The country was also gripped by a massive opium epidemic. It is little wonder why.

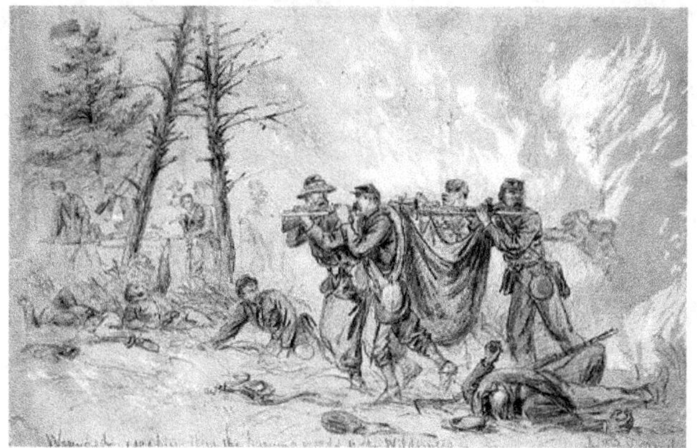

Fleeing the flames during the Battle of the Wilderness, 1864. Under Ulysses Grant the Army would never again retreat north, but instead hammer Lee in a horrible series of battles and siege over the next year.

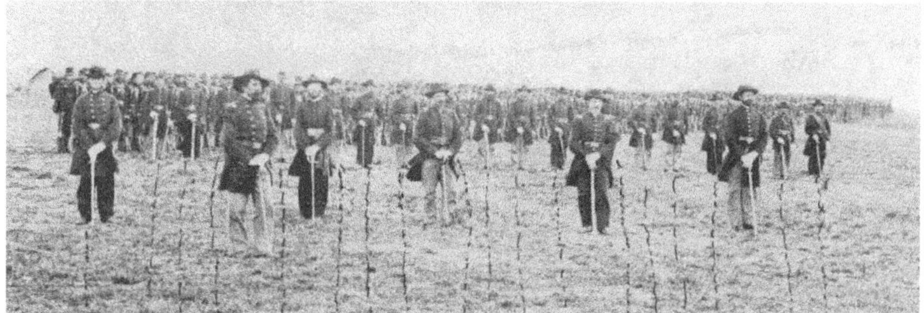

The 17th Maine near brandy Station, May 3, 1864. Once Grant set out, there would be no turning back.

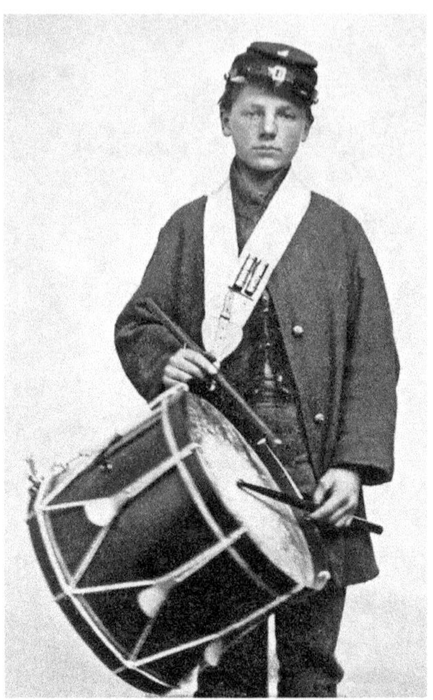

Typical Union drummer. Both armies enlisted boys as young as 12, especially in the south.

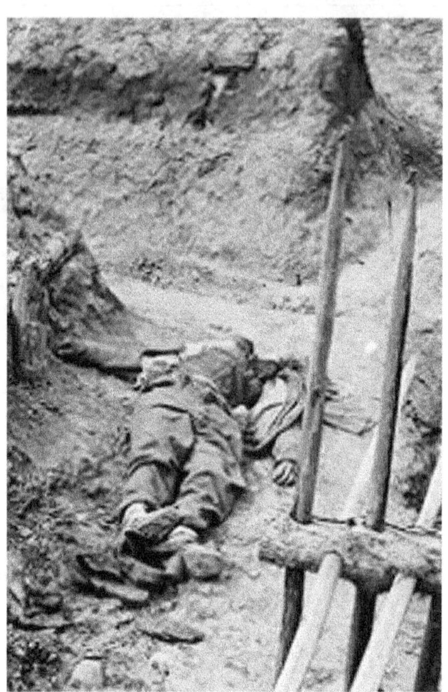

Confederate dead in the trenches of Petersburg. Lice, mud, disease, shellfire, and snipers.

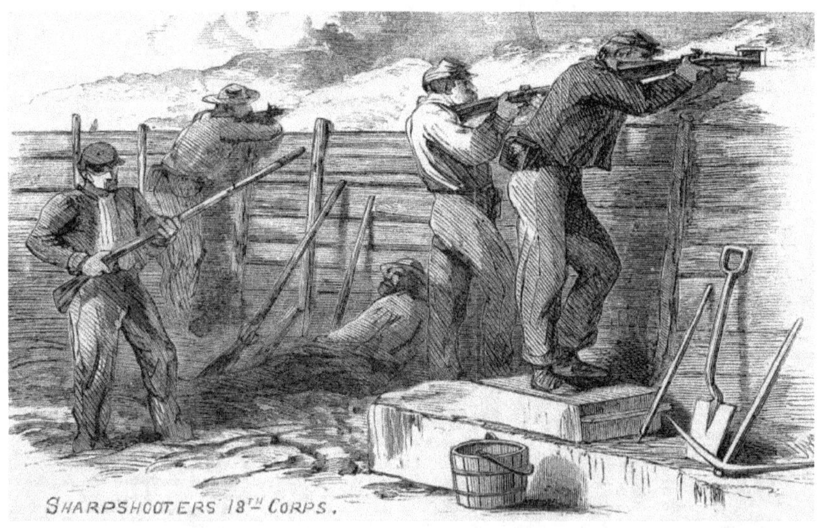

Reviled by all, sharpshooters at work in the trenches at Petersburg. The siege was a foretelling of a new war that would befall their own sons 62 years later.

Boots and Saddles

Cpl. Clarence Dudley Bartlett "Skipper"
C Troop, 12th U.S. Cavalry

Clarence Dudley Bartlett ("Skipper") was born on April 5th, 1895. His father, Frank Randle Bartlett, was a box maker at the time but would later be listed as an electrical engineer in the 1910 census. His brother Freeman was born two years later. His mother, Abbie Small Bartlett, passed away on May 28th, 1901 from childbirth complications delivering his youngest brother Isaac Henry seven days prior (puerperal septicemia). She was only 31 years old, Gramp was six. Seven years later, Frank re-married to Edna Barbour in 1908 when he was thirteen.

This is where the trajectory turned for him. Three years later he had some kind of falling out with the family, probably the step mother. So at age 16 he was "kicked out of the house." As the story goes he went to a neighbor's house. The neighbor couldn't keep him but said he had a friend in Montana he could stay with and the boy should go there and see the west "before it was gone." He bought him a ticket for Billings Montana. This would have been 1911.

He got off the train in Billings and apparently stood there looking kinda lost. Approached by the station master, he learned that the neighbor's friend had died. This had not been communicated back to Maine and it's also unclear if anyone back there had bothered to inform this friend that there was an unaccompanied minor in route to him either. Such was the state of things back then. The station master, however, knew a local hog farmer who could possibly use a hand around the farm. Calls were made and young Clarence began his new life in the "Wild West" slopping hogs and more than likely living in the barn or such.

A few months later, however, they were in town and a cattle drive was going through. Clarence somehow got in amongst the cowboys. For a boy of sixteen from the East, in that time, cowboys must have held a mythical stature. For some decades their exploits had been the raw stuff of dime novels and the infancy of film. And there Clarence was, standing amongst them on the streets of Billings.

The cowboys were apparently intrigued by his Maine accent, listened to his story and learned of his current predicament. It was said that they took pity on him and so decided to "buy" him from the hog farmer for $20 dollars, passing the hat to do so. These guys had just come off a drive so they were flush and a goodly amount of whiskey was most probably involved. I mean, they essentially purchased an indentured street urchin from a hog farmer and took him home with them out of pity and cowboy pride. The kid had come all that way to be a cowboy in the Wild West, so they made it happen. That small act had a big effect for generations to come.

They took their new charge back to the Diamond D ranch near Glendive. Over the next few years he learned how to ride and do all manner of cowboy and horsemanship things, especially trick riding. Photos of him from this time show a smiling, apparently very happy young man living the real deal cowboy experience. By all accounts he acquitted himself satisfactorily. He ultimately stayed in touch via letters with several of his ranch companions over the years.

This was the key formative time in his life and from that point forward horses and the equestrian world became the centerpiece of it, as it would also be for most of us who followed. This was where this Bartlett line decidedly went cavalry, and it's a spirit that lives on in me in a fairly prominent way.

On May 12th, 1917 he enlisted in the US army at age 22, Service # 350356. He elected service in the US Cavalry and was assigned to C Troop, 12th US Cavalry in the Panama Canal Zone through 1919, being discharged at Camp Dix NJ on October 1st of that year.

The 12th Cavalry was born on 2 February 1901 when Congress authorized the organization of the Twelfth Regiment of Cavalry, Army of the United States. Under this authority, the regiment was formed at

Fort Sam Houston, Texas on 8 February 1901. From 1901 until 1911, the regiment served at posts in Texas, Georgia, and the Philippines. Between border skirmishes with Mexican revolutionaries in Texas and scrapes with Moro insurgents in the Philippines the 12th developed a strong NCO and Junior officers corps, wise to the ways of cavalry small unit action and skirmishing. These were the men who came to be Clarence's new mentors.

In early 1916 the 1st Squadron (which contained C Troop) shipped out for duty at Corozal in the Panama Canal Zone. The squadron remained in Corozal until 1921 when the regiment was reorganized during the drawdown following the First World War. During their time there, C Troop became renowned as being "The first and only outfit to successfully hike across the Isthmus of Panama," with their horses intact. (March, 1918. C.D. Bartlett, inscription on photo) The Spanish and previous units had tried but the horses had died, most likely from Venezuelan equine encephalitis. This success was no doubt due to advances in veterinary medicine at the time, an understanding of mosquitos as a disease vector with preventative measures against, and strenuous anti mosquito efforts of the US Army Sanitation Corps.

Sometime in 1917 he was assigned to a group overseeing a transport ship of horses to France (probably from the Aleshire Remount Depot in Front Royal, VA). Upon arrival in France they were unable to dock so Clarence, then only a private, stepped up with a solution. He proposed that if they opened the doors and lowered the gang plank he could take the dominant stallion and swim the heard to the beach as they would follow him. This approach was approved, he picked the leader and rode him down the gangplank into open water with the rest of the herd following. He swam them all to the beach where they were collected up by the Quartermasters. He hitched a ride back to the ship and they returned to America. That was the sum of his involvement in the campaigns in France.

Life in Panama

By 1917 life in the Canal Zone on the military bases had been fairly well developed into modern posts with permanent buildings and stables. The quarters were mostly two story wood barracks with fully screened in windows and verandas as were the mess facilities. Stables were likewise well built with vast parade fields abounding and gun ranges scattered about. On exercise, however, the troops retained their traditional canvas tents.

Days consisted of the routine common to all militaries...eat, drill, chores, eat, more drill, more chores. In the case of the cavalry that involved hours and hours of care for the horses. Grooming, shoeing, mucking stalls, exercising, feeding or grazing, and cleaning or repairing tack. There was also rifle drill and occasional exercise of the troop's heavy weapons section which consisted of three Vickers 2.5in mountain howitzers which were disassembled and carried on mules.

For pastimes the troop had a baseball team but more especially a trick riding team. Gramp was part of both and no doubt excelled in riding considering the head start he had gotten in Montana. For this the installation had its own arena and many events were held there that mixed the classic equestrian events with rodeo, trick riding and Roman style two horse riding.

It wasn't all fun and games, however. The presence of the 12th Cavalry in force was due to the outbreak of, and impending entry of the United States into WW1. Patrolling the 553sq miles of the Canal Zone was the job of the cavalry and they spent a good deal of time doing it. Limited roads, mountainous terrain, heat, jungle, and everything in those jungles, were all their constant companions. There was a reason that the achievement of C Troop being the first to transverse the Isthmus with their horses intact was a celebrated event.

A large part of the hazard was Yellow fever, a tropical disease spread by the Aëdes Aegypti mosquito. It carries a fairly high fatality rate and is debilitating to anyone who contracts it. Fortunately for the men of 1st Squadron, 12th Cavalry vast measures had been taken to control the pest by the Army Sanitation Commission led by Dr. William Crawford Gorgas. In the age before DEET, however, bugs in the zone remained a constant source of irritation for troops especially in the field and away from installations.

Another was the general unrest that had always plagued the region. This was the early 20th century and things weren't always done in the spirit of fairness, especially when it came to indigenous peoples of the region. While not endemic, flare ups of violence did occur. The Army would of course have been called upon to deal with it. It was told to me over the years that during one of these flare ups with local Indians Gramp was wounded by an arrow while protecting some kind of survey or work crew. If this was true, it didn't affect his affinity for native peoples that he carried with him throughout all his life.

He made promotion to NCO, one of the only Bartletts to do so. On April 21st, 1919 he made Lance Corporal and in June of that year made full Corporal. That would have put him in charge of a section of six or so troopers.

Finally, on October 1st, 1919 he was honorably discharged from the Army at Ft. Dix, NJ. He returned home and on March 20th, 1920 married Madge Storey. He was 25, she 21. In 1923 they had my father, William Storey Bartlett.

The Bartlett School of Equitation

Upon returning home from the service, he naturally gravitated towards equine circles, eventually making horses his life's work. Over the years he built up the "Bartlett School of Equitation" in Brunswick and later Naples, which served Maine's extensive summer camp and private school network with horses and equestrian program management. He also ran the riding programs at a few private schools such as Oak Grove Coburn in East Vasselboro, ME.

As dad was growing up, Clarence, now known as "Skipper," would periodically procure a load of mustangs and surplus cavalry remounts for the schools. They would go to the railhead in Portland and take delivery of the horses. The cavalry remounts were excellent school horses as they had already seen their share of inexperienced riders, motorized machines and loud noises. They would sprinkle the remounts amongst the mustangs, who had never experienced any of the above. The whole crew would then mount up and start riding towards Brunswick or Naples.

The first part of the journey was always exciting as the mustangs were getting their first look at things like cars and trucks, which in the horse brain were probably equated somewhere between grizzly bears and dragons. All kinds of terror would break out alongside the remounts, who were probably casting sideways glances at their wild cousins and chuckling. The presence of the remounts, who didn't seem to fear the monsters, had a steadying effect on the mustangs and by the time the journey ended they were usually calm and accustomed to the strange sights. From there they would start their new lives as school horses for children.

There was also an incident at Bowdoin College during the time he was teaching riding there I was told of. A student fell of the roof of one of the dormitories and was paralyzed from the waist down. For some reason Gramp through that he could fix it. Every afternoon he would hoist the kid up onto a cavalry saddle, secure his legs to the stirrups and walk him around the ring for an hour or so. He recalled the boy would ride with tears running down his face. He did this and in about four months the kid regained feeling and use of his legs. Whatever need to move, flex and thus heal apparently did so. It may sound farfetched, but that kind of injury is not uncommon with mounted troops or cowboys. It's very possible that he picked up on it there.

I knew Grampa "Skipper" Bartlett as a child and have clear memory of him. The home and stable was in Naples by then. The home was a typical two story Maine home with a finished basement. The basement was where all of Gramp's memorabilia and books were, centered on a large brick fireplace. There was any and all manner of Native American items and books, some of which I still have.

He was a big fan of Louis L'Mour novels of the old west. There was also a basket of toy cowboy and indian figures, which I played with when we came to visit weekly. He and Nana had traveled quite a bit and he had a collection of Royal Canadian Mounted Police posters and objects from a trip to Canada, a few of which I still have. It's easy to see why he admired the RCMPs, in their red uniforms and big Hanoverian horses. He also had numerous Native American objects, for he never lost the affinity and respect for them he got from his time in Montana. These were hugely fascinating things for the 10 and 11 year old me during that time.

The stable was a long structure with stalls and tack rooms down both sides. By the time I came along there were not so many horses as he was old and retired by then, but my older siblings spent many summers riding there. At my age of the time it was a vast structure that smelled of hay and saddle leather with secret rooms full of interesting objects. Out back was a riding ring, surrounded by huge pine trees that stretched up to the heavens. I was told as a youngster that they were "Kings" pine, because before the Revolution an inspector for the Royal Navy would walk the woods and score them with the broad arrow of the British quartermaster. They were ideal for masts on sailing ships. Red squirrels abounded.

There was also a grey 1946 Ford 8N tractor. He had waited until after WW2 ended to buy it so it would be delivered with rubber tires. He used it to groom the ring and for other small chores. It came to live with us after his passing and then it came down to me. It still runs and finally needed new tires after 50 something years. As of this writing it's with my friend Scott, in southern Virginia, who works his wood lots and gardens with it. This year it needed new rings. 74 year old tractor.

12th U.S. Cavalry Armaments and Organization

Armaments
1911 Colt Automatic Pistol .45 ACP
1903 Springfield Rifle .30-06
Model 1913 "Patton" Cavalry Sabre
Quick Firing 2.95in Vickers Mountain Gun, deployed on pack mules.

Organization
12th Cavalry Regt consisted of three squadrons 1-3
Each Squadron contained 5-6 Troops (1st Squadron A-E, 2nd squadron F-L and a HQ Squadron of heavy weapons and supply / medical)
An individual cavalry troop consisted of five officers, 105 men and 260 horses (three mounts per trooper).

* At the time individual squadrons would be assigned on detached service from the main regiment, hence the 1st going to Panama.

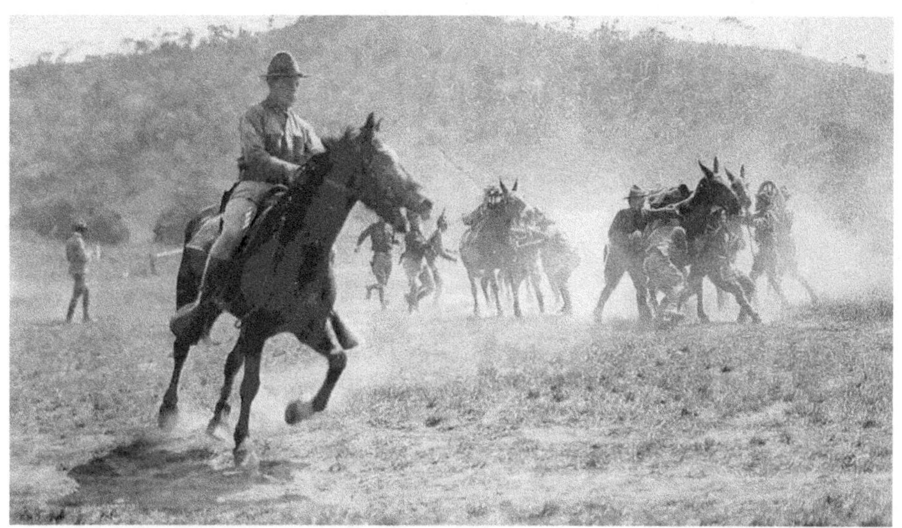

The mountain gun section of C Troop 12th Cavalry exercising on the range at Corazol, Panama Canal Zone 1917.

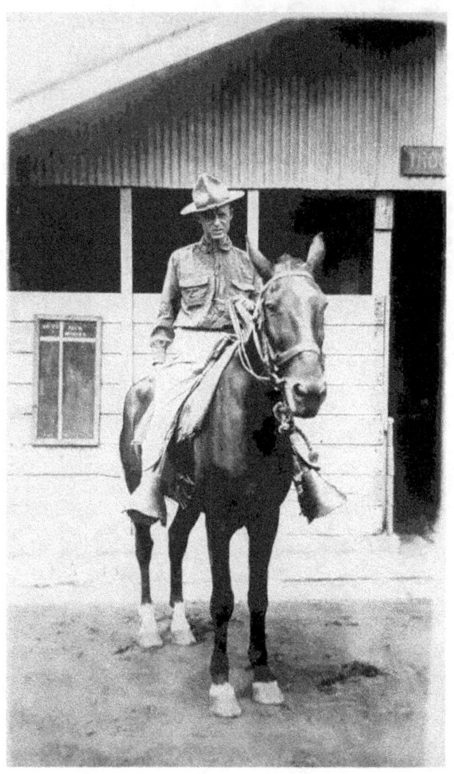

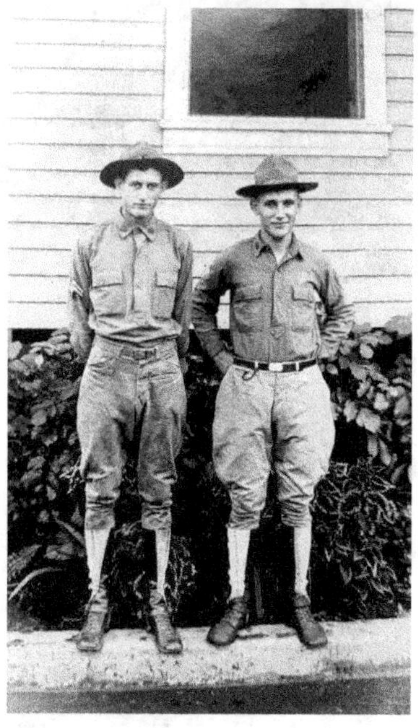

Clarence Dudley Bartlett, Panama Canal zone 1916-1918. Hot and humid, but a good posting overall.

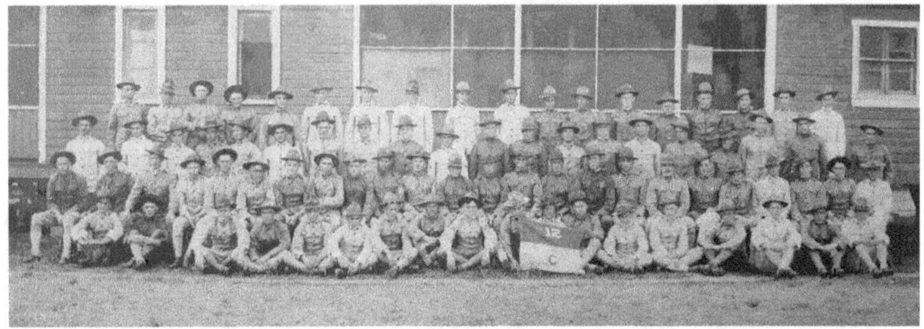

"Troop C 12th Cav at Corozol CZ Panama. March 1918. The first and only outfit to successfully hike across the Isthmus of Panama. C.D. Bartlett." Postcard inscription on the back of the photo. (back row, 4th from L)

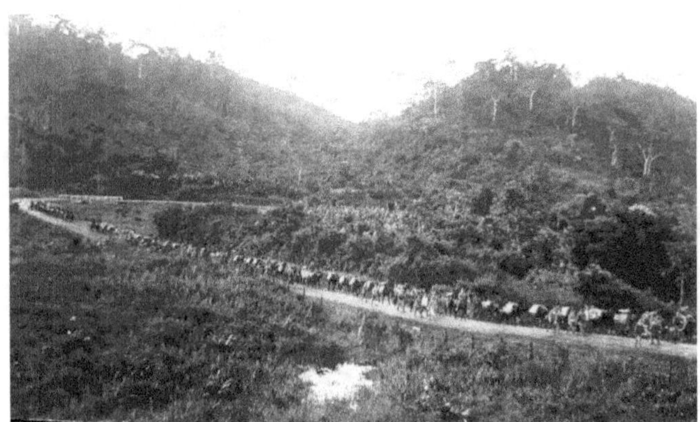

C Troop on the move, Panama. The tropical climate and disease had decimated earlier attempts to move horse units across the country.

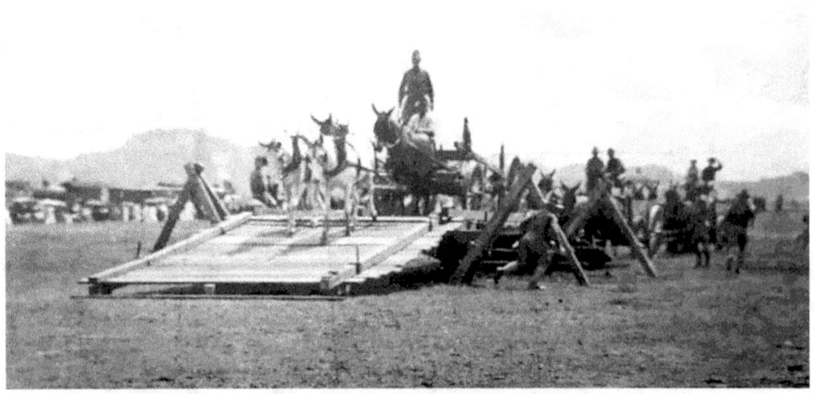

Bridging exercise to bring the wagons and mules over.

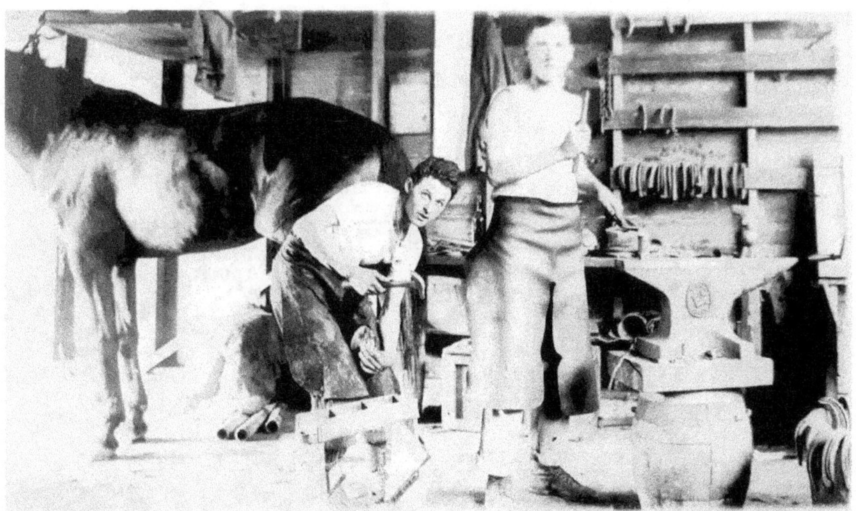

Gramp (L) in the farriers shop, Panama Canal Zone. While mobile and capable of moving across rough terrain, horse cavalry comes at a price...endless hours of caring for and maintaining horses.

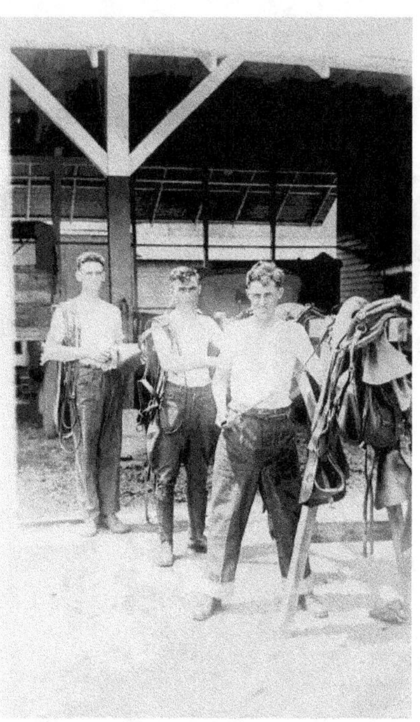

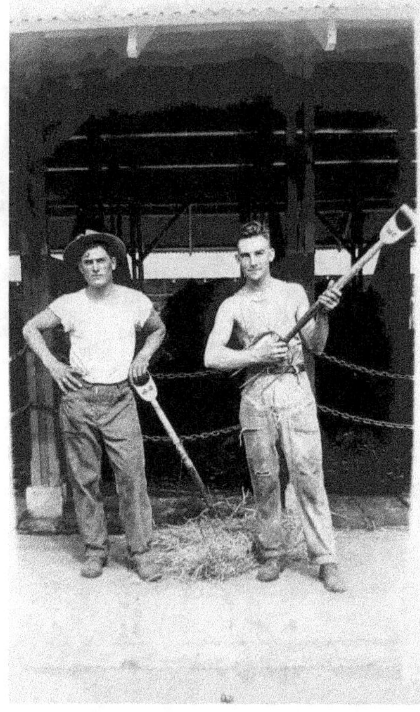

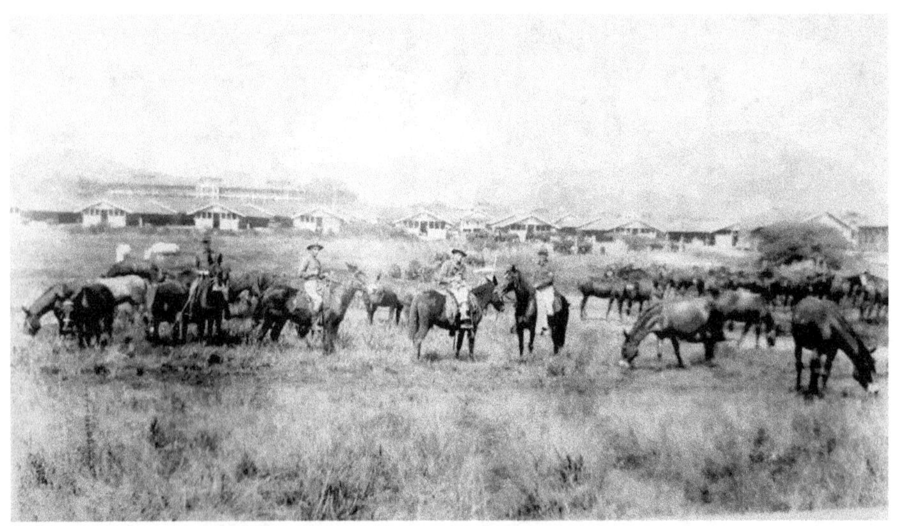

Grazing the remount herd behind the stables.

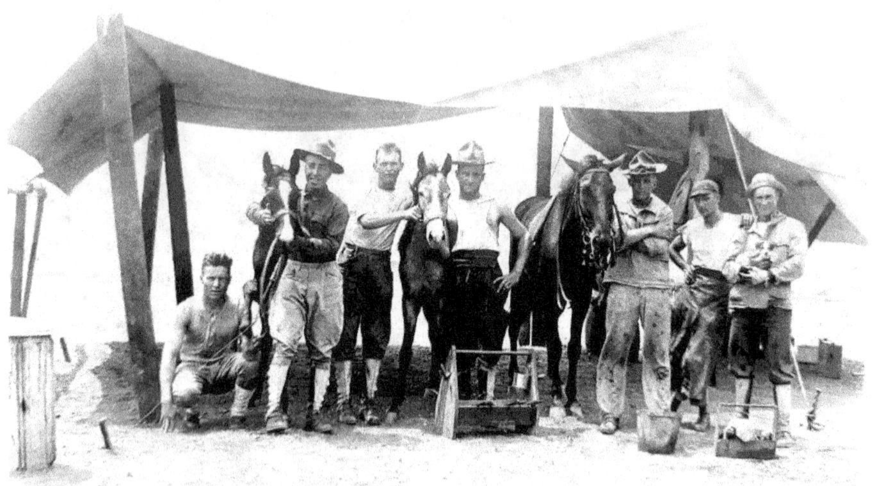

Farrier station under canvas in the field.

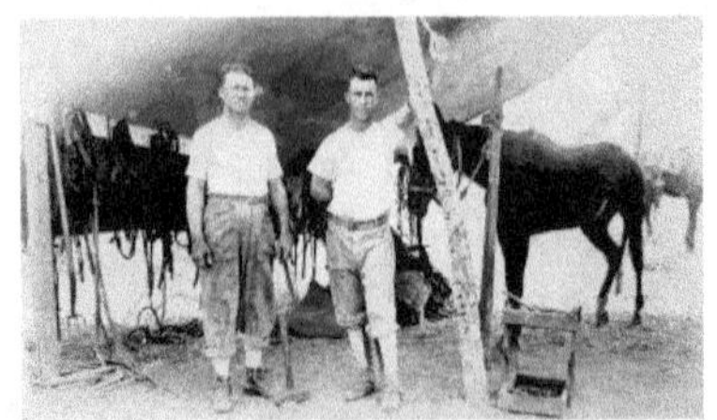

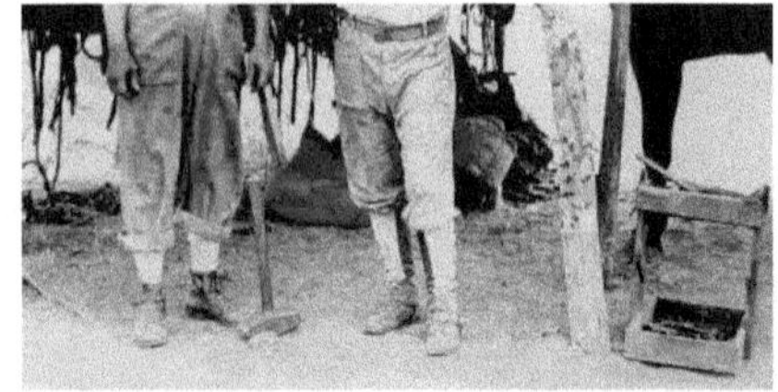

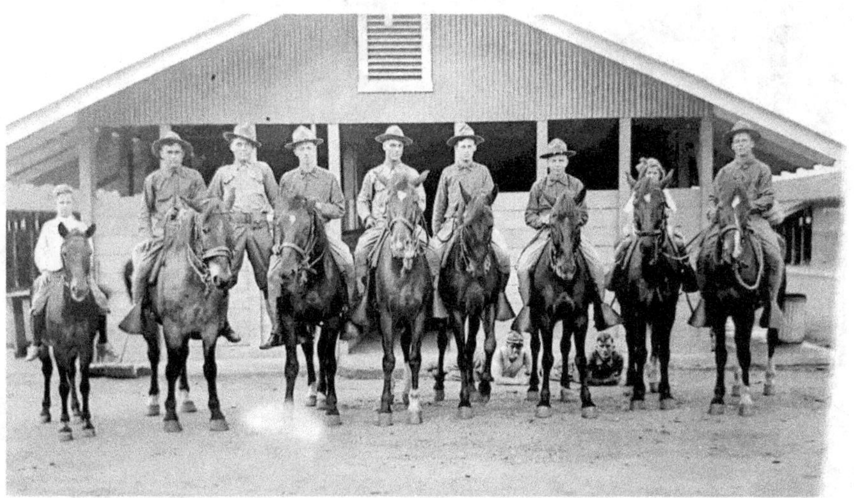

Gramps section outside their stables. Note the children. Most likely belonging to officers or senior NCOs. They managed to find the one boy a pony.

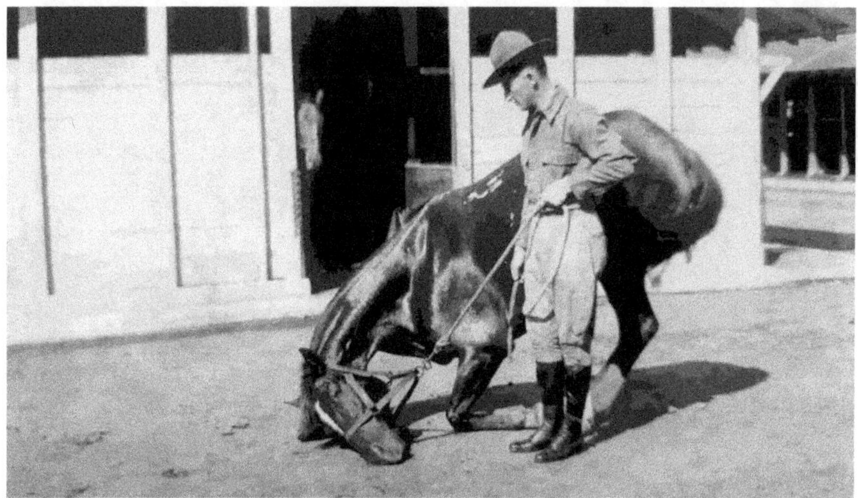

Training horses for show and trick riding was especially common. Not only did it enhance the equitation skills of the troopers, but in the age before electronic entertainment, provided for a useful distraction that filled dual purpose.

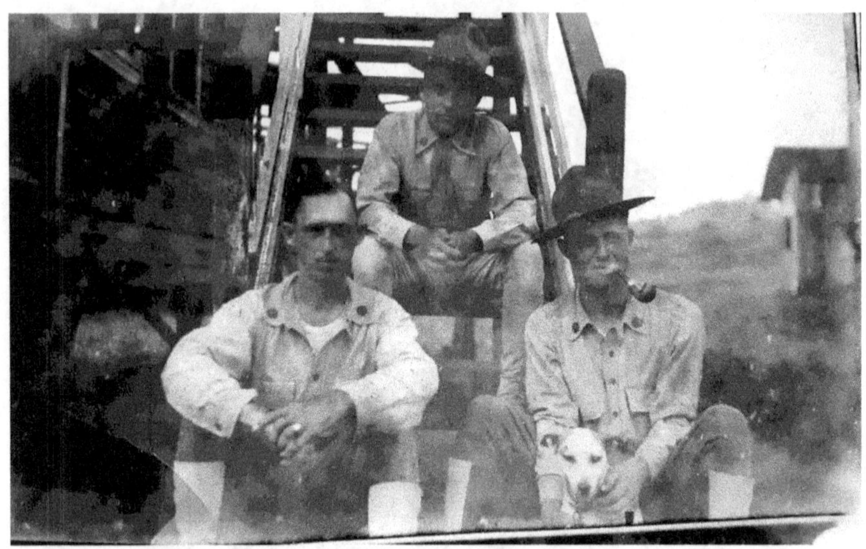

Gramp, on the right, with the Troop's mascot. Older now, a corporal, and smoking a pipe, which he would do for the rest of his life.

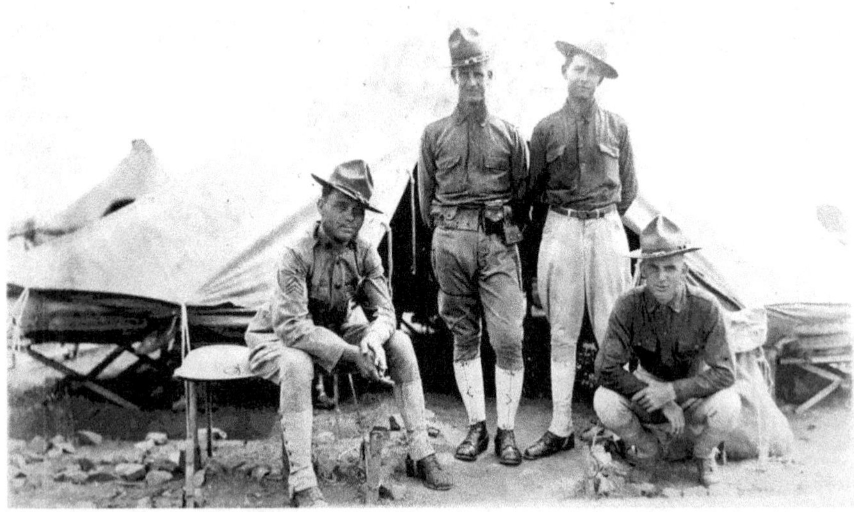

Gramp's section tenting in the field under canvas. Despite their distance from the war in France, the strategic importance of the Panama Canal meant that U.S. troops had to maintain a fairly high state of readiness to respond to not only any threat inside the Canal Zone, but in the neighboring republics as well.

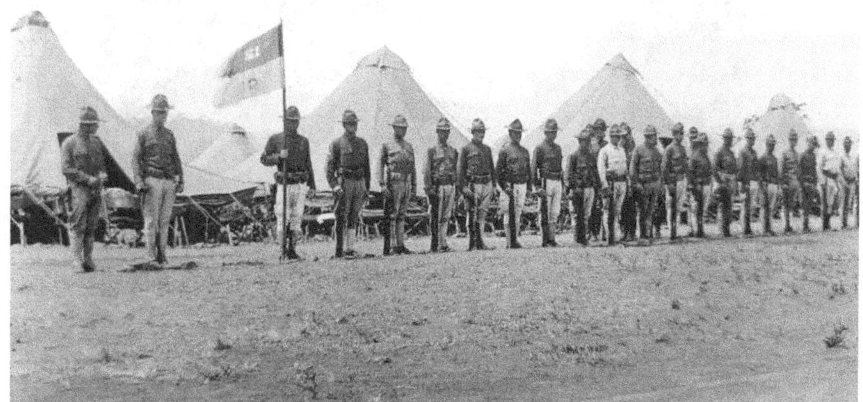

Even in the field, drill and parade made up a daily part of a Trooper's life.

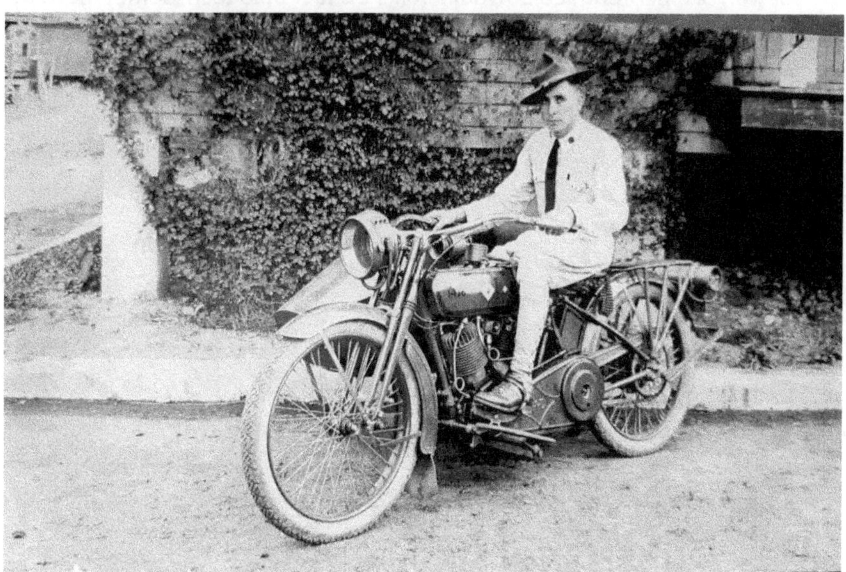

An early Harley Davidson, as the first motorized vehicles were introduced. They couldn't know it at the time but this was the beginning of the end of horse mounted cavalry. By 1943 the tank, truck, and scout car became the mobility of the cavalry. Gramp's son would attend the last parade at Ft. Riley, KS just before shipping off to his generation's war.

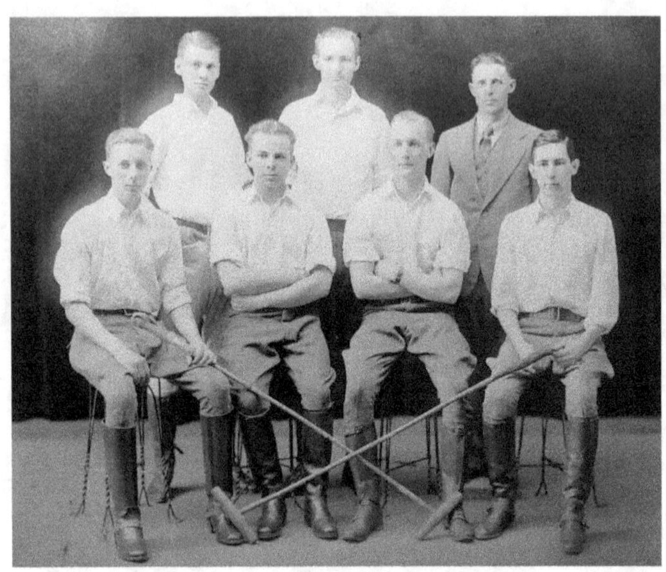

Post war, Skipper founded Bowdoin College's first polo team sometime in the 1920s. He became a major influence in the Maine equestrian industry.

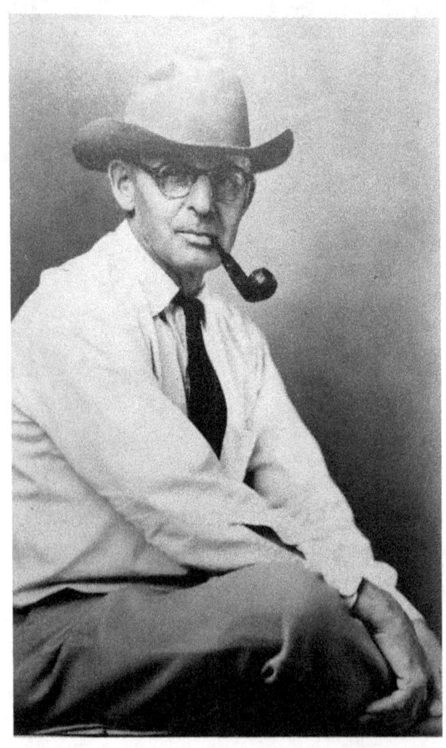

You Can Give Your Heart to Jesus, But Your Ass Belongs to The Corps.

PFC William S. Bartlett

Easy Co. 2/7 Marines. 1st MARDIV

Dad was born on May 31st, 1923 to Madge Storey and Skipper Bartlett. By then Skipper (Gramp) was running a horse operation in Brunswick. They lived on Thompson Street.

Life was not terribly soft, as this was the age of "Spare the rod, spoil the child," and Skipper rarely spared the rod. In today's day and age we would probably balk at how unsparingly he was with it. I can only remember five or six times when Dad ever spanked me for anything, even then it was half hearted. I guess those memories didn't jibe well with him and he didn't carry on that tradition.

He adored his grandfather William H. Storey, by all accounts. Storey is listed as a "Teamster" at 25 Jordan Ave in the Brunswick Directory of 1910, but by 1923 was running a large lumber and ice operation in the area. At one time they had seven portable, steam powered saw mills going, employed 300 men and were working 56 draft animals. So dad grew up around these lumbermen and animals.

A Generation Hardened: The Great Depression

Dad was 6 years old when the Stock Market crashed in 1929 and the following Depression indelibly shaped his life, as it did for his entire generation. There was no escaping the grim realities of it once it really dug in during the early and mid-thirties.

Growing up in Maine, at that time, provided more than a few adventures for the young boy. His grandfather William Storey, for example, had his big logging and ice operation which was a bustling concern. For a boy of six to ten years old this was pretty big stuff and he had a front row seat for it as his father Clarence was working part time for the outfit as a teamster in those early days of marriage and family.

There was one occasion he told of where he was riding back from school on his mule. (Yes, he rode a mule to a one room school in Brunswick. This has been confirmed!) It was the end of the day and the men had parked a couple of the steam engines on the side of the road. Well, the mule balked at them and refused to pass. Dad proceeded to cuss up a storm about how his "Goddamned mule" wouldn't go past the engines. This amused the teamsters, from whom he had learned these words, to no end so they hitched up a full team and moved the engine to the other side of the road, at which point the mule passed. This was no small endeavor, as harnessing, hitching, and un-harnessing at least four draft horses probably took at least a couple hours.

On other occasions during the summer he would go into the lumber camps to do odd jobs like cleaning the tack and learning to drive the log and lumber sledges. During my childhood we were on our way up to the Allagash River, driving along the Kennebec in the late 70s. The last log drive was taking place, as they halted the practice because the pine bark was acidifying the river. He told me to take a close look because "you'll never see that again." We later stopped by the Patten Lumberman's Museum and he pointed out all of the various bits and pieces of equipment from those days. He related that Grampa Storey kept all 300 of his men working during the Depression until he was no longer able to feed them, at which point his operation came to an end.

Then there was the ice wagon incident. Back in those days home refrigeration came in the form of blocks of ice, delivered by wagon weekly. This was part of the larger Maine industry that Grampa Storey worked. (Maine ice was actually one of the major U.S. exports during those days, shipping to as far away as India.) Each block was cut and weighed by the ice man and there were always chips of ice on the wagon's tailgate. In the summer, as the ice man would pass, the neighborhood children would run out and grab these chips. So of course dad does this too. But Gramp felt that this was stealing somehow and forbid him to do it. Being a kid he did it anyway and caught a hell of a whipping for it. As aforementioned, Gramp did not spare the rod.

There would be other times, such as his forbidden visits to the "Hobo Jungle." As the Depression ground on, veritable armies of men wandered the country by rail looking for work. Areas outside the rail yards became their camping spots and became known as "Jungles." All this is very interesting to young people, of course, and they would go down into these areas to visit. Mind you, these were simply unemployed men, not the kind of sketchy people you find around rail yards today. They would cook communally and share their hobo soups with the young visitors.

Gramp, being Gramp, took exception to these visits and forbid them. Dad, being Dad, disregarded the injunction. So the day soon came when Gramp went looking for him, armed with a coach whip, and found him down in the Jungle. Now mind you, Gramp is an expert with this, and as he chased Dad along the rail siding the whip would strike out with a crack, each time causing the young transgressor to howl. The hobos thought this hilarious and every time the whip cracked they broke out in peals of laughter that Dad never forgot.

On another occasion, probably in the mid-30s, Dad and several of his friends thought it would be glamourous to "Ride the rods" on a rail car as the hobos did. These were appendages underneath a rail car known as braking beams, small wooden platforms under a boxcar or carriage where the nimble could climb aboard as a train left a yard and ride to the next destination, laying down on them. So he and his friends waited for a south bound freight out of Brunswick and hopped on. They soon found out how dangerous a business this is and bailed out at the Portland rail yard, calling to Gramp to admit what he had done and request a ride home. He asked me, when telling the story, "You know why the center of the tracks are brown? Because of all the hobos who crap themselves they're so scared down there. I never did that again."

Through all this, however, he was becoming an accomplished horseman, taking numerous ribbons since a young age and learning the trick riding art from his father. As the Depression dented but did not destroy the summer camp industry, Grampa Skipper was able to grow his equestrian school during that time.

Dad continued to go to school which was just up from a very tight turn on one of the local roads. At the time there were no snow plows and cars were still not as widespread as they are today. Hence, people would get around in winter with sleighs pulled by horses. To facilitate this the towns employed giant snow rollers to compact the snow which were pulled by teams of up to thirteen horses. That one turn, however, would always hang it up. Well, Dad appeared one day around lunch and asked the snow roller man to let him have a go, which he did, and successfully wheeled the team around the corner. Thereafter, whenever the snow roller man would come with the team he would stop there, repair for a cup of coffee, and send a runner to fetch dad. He would come down and wheel the team around the corner.

Learning to drive a car, however, did not go as smoothly. At the time Gramp had a Model-T truck and was teaching Dad to drive it. Early in this process Dad let slip the clutch and stomped the gas. The Model T launched forward across the ring, coming to be lodged between two pine trees. He had it wedged in so tightly they had to break out the saws and take down one of the trees to free it. I still maintain that he was better with horses than he ever was with machines.

Dad also had a mischief streak, as may be evidenced by the previously mentioned escapades. At one point he was sent off to attend Gould Academy, a college prep boarding school in Bethel, ME that had been there since 1836. One can imagine it was a fairly uptight place to be. In short order he tested those boundaries and was caught smoking cigarettes. Back to Naples on the next bus for him. If you look at pictures of him from that time he has that little grin and gleam in his eye of the mischief joker. As war clouds gathered in Europe and the Pacific, that was about to change forever.

Boots and Saddles: The Last of the Cavalry

In the run up to WW2 Dad set off for university, intending to study veterinary medicine. He was accepted and went off to Michigan State. He enrolled in the ROTC program, then known as the 3655th Service Unit, on December 3rd, 1942. His service number was 16105014 and he was assigned to Company C of the Engineer Detachment for roster purposes, as they did not have an official Cavalry unit. It was apparently unofficially run in partnership with the equestrian program. It was kind of a "Cavalry Club." He was issued the 1941 edition of The ROTC Advanced Manual for Cavalry, which I grew up with and still have. (This was the book that taught me how to read maps, utilize scouting and patrolling tactics, and gave me a bunch of time tested, basic soldiering skills.)

There was lots of riding, polo skirmishes and gymkhana for them. As his undergraduate classes rolled by and as he passed his pre-med courses for the veterinary medicine he enrolled in the "Army Specialized Training: Veterinary Medicine" program in September of 1942. This included a number of trips for exercises to Ft. Riley, Kansas where the 9th U.S. Cavalry was stationed at the army's Cavalry School.

But with America now fully involved in Europe and the Pacific, and with the incoming supremacy of the motorized and tank forces, the horse service was fading. Sometime in the fall of 1943 the cadets got word to get down to Riley for the last parade. The 9th was shipping out to North Africa and there would be one last pass in review with the horses. They knew that this was it, the horse cavalry was over. Every mount, every trooper, every flag and piece of equipment was brought out. The review lasted the better part of the entire day. He told me that by the end of it you could see where tears had tracked through the dust on the faces of the older troopers. This was the end of the horse soldiers. "I thank god they don't take horses onto battlefields anymore. At the same time there is something special, a bond between a cavalryman and his horse that no longer exists. It was a sad day," he recalled.

Things were about to get sadder. The Army would be ending the AST Veterinary Medicine program that June. Cadets who wished could enter Federal Service with the USDA as meat inspectors in the slaughter houses. As Dad recalled, "There was no way in hell I was going to do that."

So in the spring of 1944 he was home on break and was visiting cousins and friends in Brunswick. All the recruiting offices were along Main St at that time and they were all down there walking past them. One by one they went into the separate stations. One, Charlie, went into the Army Air Corps. He would become a tail gunner on a B-25 Mitchell and was shot down over Burma by the Japanese, never to be seen again. They never found the wreckage. Freeman joined the Navy and went to the Atlantic on a sub chaser. Robert, who had joined early on, ended up at Pointe Du Hoc with the 2nd Rangers at Normandy. Dad walked into the U.S. Marine Corps office.

Because he was a volunteer, he could pick his military specialty. He chose aviation, as a tail gunner. They drew up a contract and sent him back to Michigan to await orders. They were not long in coming. On June 24th, 1944 he officially entered the United State Marine Corps, Service# 932541, and shipped out to the 7th Recruit Battalion, Paris Island, SC.

Your Ass Belongs to the Corps

When he arrived at the island, the personnel officers looked at his contract and exclaimed, "Aerial gunner?! Who the hell wrote this?! We ain't got no aerial gunners anymore. But ahhhh…it says here you were a Cavalry cadet. Well, you're in luck, we do have a need for Scout Observers in the infantry." Bam…0636 Scout Observer / 0890 Photo Interpreter. Goodbye blue skies, hello mud and blood.

Paris Island 1944 was a bustling place. Replacing the massive losses of the Pacific Campaigns was in full swing. Drill Instructors and training cadre were made up of the survivors of those campaigns. They were hard men, they had seen the brutality of facing the Japanese adversary, and their job was to prepare recruits to face the same. The training was savage, none of the niceties we see today.

The drill field was a particular place of torture, with the temperatures of the South Carolina summer routinely topping out over 100. One example he related was how when a marine would pass out, the instructors had the rest of the company march over the top of him. If you stepped over they made you lie down next to him and run the circuit again. Lesson? You do not stop for wounded or dead, you keep moving, because if you don't, you're going down next.

Another hellish trick was to come along and suddenly smash your fingers with a swagger stick that had a 30.06 cartridge on the end while you were standing at Port Arms. If you dropped your weapon they beat you with it. Dirty rifle? Open the action, insert your thumb and have the drill instructor slam it forward for you. Lesson? Never drop your weapon, ever, and keep it clean always. "I made each of those mistakes precisely once," he told me. "There were occasions where the blood just ran down my fingers onto my boots, but you had to stand there and take it. It was harsh, but they knew where we were headed. There was one recruit in my company who actually died and several ran." This is my rifle. There are many like it, but this one is mine...

This went on for 16 weeks.

With the hell of the island behind him, he reported to the Headquarters and Service Company, Schools Regt. Camp Lejeune NC, in October of 1944 for an additional twelve weeks of "Combat Intelligence School." Eight weeks Combat Intelligence and four weeks of Aerial Photo Interpretation. After the island this was a relief and they spent their time learning the finer points of scouting, camouflage, tactical field sketching, communication and photo interpretation. He excelled at it, as most of these tasks were the basic skills of a Cavalryman, which he was already well versed in.

Pendleton and Oceanside

After a short leave back in Maine, he shipped out to Camp Pendleton, CA Oceanside in January of 1945 to the 46th Replacement Draft (an organization that housed unassigned replacement troops headed for the Pacific). Here there would be four more months of training while the Generals and Admirals rebuilt the 1st Marine Division, shattered the previous year at Peleliu, and prepared for the next offensive move against Imperial Japan. (Fortunately for Dad, he arrived just as 5th MARDIV was being shipped out. A month earlier and he could have wound up on Iwo. Not that Okinawa was going to be any better.)

Pendleton and Oceanside had seen rapid and massive expansion since purchase of the land, the 122,798-acre Rancho Santa Margarita y Las Flores, in February 1942. On it they built the primary amphibious warfare school for the US Marine Corps, with 17 miles of oceanfront in which to train. By January of 1945 it was a permanent base with fixtures such as Quonset Huts, chow halls, base housing, administrative buildings, and vast firing ranges. Here is where the replacement drafts would be put through their paces in Amtraks, landing craft, up and down embarkation nets, and even submarines for the unlucky combat intelligence scouts.

"They loaded us up in that thing one night and headed out into the bay. They called 'em pig boats because they stank, and this one sure did, all those guys cooped up in there," he recalled of his submarine experience. "It was an old boat. No sooner did they dive than this thing starts leaking, and creaking, and groaning. Little water jets started spraying out from the joints of the pipes, and we were like 'What the hell, it's gonna sink!"

"They finally surfaced a few miles off shore and we went up through the forward hatch and inflated these rubber rafts and had to paddle in for a night reconnaissance. It was a long haul to shore but I've never been so glad to be out of a boat in my life. I never wanted to go down in one of those things ever again," he concluded.

Leaking submarines and ocean surf were not the only dangers the replacement draft faced. One day the Captain in charge of his replacement company came and said he needed some volunteers for a work detail on the other side of the base. Well, one of the things they tell you is never volunteer for anything, so no one immediately jumped up. The captain spoke again and said that the scouts in particular might want to jump in on this. Dad and his guys kinda looked at each other curiously and the Captain spelled it out. "The Amphibious Recon guys are coming around today and they're gonna be looking for scouts to 'Volunteer' for the Raider Battalions. So who wants on this work detail?" Every scout in the sections hand went up.

"We spent the rest of the day scrubbing trash cans for his friend on the other side of the post and we felt that was a fair deal," he said. "They'd have Shanghai'd us for sure." Raider Battalions had the distinct Marine Corps honor of being inserted from submarines, at night, onto isolated, Japanese held islands to knock out radio stations and such. Their casualty and capture rates (read; executed by Samurai sword) were enormous. Dodged another one.

"Report back here, ready to sail across gods vast ocean, where we will meet our enemy, and kill them all."
Chesty Puller

Sometime in late April 1945 the young, green, "Boots" of the 46th Replacement Draft boarded ships at San Diego and sailed west towards the setting sun. The exact vessel Dad sailed on has been lost to history, but he was sure that it was a 414ft Liberty Ship.

He related how they were stacked 8 high in bunks down in the hold and they would step all over each other getting into and out of the bunks. He was convinced that had they been torpedoed nobody would have been able to get out. They were allowed to take a shower and only got 1 minute of fresh, hot water, but unlimited cold sea water. So they showered with the seawater and rinsed with the fresh. They served shit on a shingle almost every day. Long boring days of endless ocean. That would soon change, however, as they were headed for the Battle of Okinawa.

Welcome to Hell

The 46th Replacement Draft came ashore in early May, landing sometime around May 10th with 25 officers and 653 enlisted men. Fighting had been going on since April 1st when the first landings had been carried out by the largest invasion fleet in history. Initially, the landing forces struck out across the island, cutting it in half and taking two airfields at Yontan and Kadeana.

The first day he and another guy were told to dig foxholes. They scraped out a little ditch because it was hard ground, but not much more. Then the Kamikazes came in. Every gun in the fleet opened up. Some of the flak had time or altitude fuses, but not the 40 and 20mm. It all started coming down around them, exploding. They burrowed into the coral like woodchucks and the guy with him defecated himself. "You never seen two men dig a hole so fast in your life, we were scared shitless," he told me.

At one point they were down on the shore when a Kamikaze, hit but not destroyed, crash landed. The pilot survived and swam to shore. He emerged from the water dressed in his funeral kimono, painted face, etc. He looked like an, "apparition out of medieval Japan. He couldn't have been more than 16 or 17. We were dumbstruck, but a SGT was kind of hanging back. When he saw that we were Marines he tried to pull a pistol and the SGT cut him in half with a Thompson. That was my first taste of war in the Pacific."

Baptism of Fire

Shortly thereafter, Dad got picked to go with a swarm of replacements up into the Motobo Peninsula, which had been taken earlier in the campaign by the 6th Marine Division. It had been a nasty fight in six-square-miles around and on the 1,200-foot mass of Mount Yae Take. The Japanese commander, Colonel Takesiko Udo and his *Kunigami Detachment* went into prepared defensive positions; steep ravines, heavy with jungle and honeycombed with interconnecting tunnels. All of this bristled with mortars, heavy artillery, 20mm Flak, machine guns, suicidal Japanese infantry, and liberally seeded with land mines. They fought to the death, it was a mess, and a taste of what was in store when the allied forces headed south.

Plenty of stragglers and hold outs remained, however, as the area had only been taken two weeks prior. Great place to break in replacements. Dad recalled that they went through the ravines littered with Japanese dead, bayoneting bodies or shooting them in the head to ensure they were actually dead. A few sprayed blood when shot, indicating that they had been playing dead, waiting for the Marines to pass before shooting. As they went about clearing caves he acquired a Thompson sub machinegun. As a scout they made him approach the entrances to the caves. He would stick it around the corner and spray. Engineers would then come up, torch it with a flame thrower, and seal the entrance with a satchel charge. The stench of decomposing bodies was overpowering.

With the Old Breed

"Japs are fighting for their own turf now. Every step we go south they're gonna get meaner and meaner." Merriell "Snafu" Shelton, K/3/5th Marines.

They did the Motobo shakedown cruise for about a week before higher pushed them down to the southern line to refill the Marine units who'd taken a blooding on Dakashi Ridge. This is where he fell in with Easy Company, 2nd Battalion, 7th Marines sometime on May 17th.

What he joined was a severely tested rifle company that had fought to take the ridge since the 10th under accurate and intense enemy artillery and mortar fire. At the same time they were contending with the usual suicidal resistance of Japanese in spider holes and tunnels, each one having to be reduced through close assaults. Total casualties for the regiment at Dakashi were 110 killed, 884 wounded. The Japanese shelling had been so complete and intense that the Marines had been ordered to not to retrieve their dead as they were losing men making the attempts. There are few things the Maine Corps will guarantee you, but the one thing they promise is to retrieve your remains if you are killed. That they would suspend this practice is indicative of how desperate the situation was. Between Japanese and Marine dead laying everywhere, maggots quickly overran the entire battle area.

So imagine for a moment what that must have felt like to arrive into that as a replacement. The 7th had been horrendously battered at Peleliu in 1944. The survivors went back to the island base of Pavuvu and rebuilt the regiment with replacement drafts. These guys have been together for months and they've just fought another terrible battle. Now you show up. A fresh faced "boot" from stateside. Nobody trusts you and nobody wants to know you because you're probably going to be dead before they can commit your name to memory. You've walked some miles through a devastated, WW1-esque landscape. There's dead people everywhere, just like on Motobo, but on a vaster scale. You are now surrounded by strangers.

He was immediately thrown into the fight for Wana Ridge, which had been bleeding the 7th Marines for the better part of a week as they came down off Dakashi and tried to take the northwestern side. Back and fourth, up and down, steadily losing men, until finally relieved on the 19th. The whole place was zeroed by artillery on Shuri Heights and laced with tunnels and spider holes. Okinawa had been the Japanese Army's artillery school. They knew every inch of it.

This was also about the time he caught a piece of mortar fragment from a Jap knee mortar in the hand. He walked for god knows how far back to a forward field hospital where they had tents set up and a ward. Taking a seat on a cot he waited for the corpsman to come through. When he got to dad he set his instrument tray down on a small table and turned to work on the man next to him. Dad reached over, took up a scalpel and dug the chunk of Jap metal out of his hand. "He turned to me and said, 'Hey, you can't do that!' And I said, 'Well, I just did, gimme that iodine." He doused his hand, wrapped it in a bandage and left, grabbing a box of K-Rations on the way out and walked back to the line. He tended to his own wound care with the corpsman on the line and never did go back to the FH.

He was never entered into the hospital records as he didn't hang around long enough so he was never put in for a Purple Heart. Getting hit and then subsequently returning to his unit with food, however, no doubt put him in better stead with the veterans. No longer a "Boot" new guy. No small thing in that hellscape.

And then it started raining. Biblical levels of Pacific rain. The storms started on May 20th and went through to the 29th. It turned the island into a sea of mud like something out of the worst of WW1. Tanks, trucks and Amtracs bogged down, useless. Only a few roads remained functional.

During this time Dad and his comrades were squatting in the mud waiting on replacements and supplies. There was a convoy of trucks who were supposed to be coming up with food and drinking water. With so many dead around, nothing on the island could be touched. It all had to come up from the rear in 5 gallon jerry cans, but there was no sign of the trucks. So the scout section was told to go back to the road, 2 miles away, and find the trucks. He said the mud was up to their knees in most places. After a long slog across the mire they came upon a column of maybe a half dozen trucks, stalled out on the side of the road. Upon closer inspection they found the operators cowering in the mud of the ditch while a lone Japanese soldier with a burned out machine gun fired an odd round a couple times a minute from a cave he had hidden in.

"This shell shocked Jap would yank and yank on it and then he would get off a shot," he recalled. "The barrel was burned out so it would go 'Pop! Plook!' maybe a couple dozen yards away. Well, he had these drivers terrified. They were colored support troops and they told us, 'You boys are front line, we can't get in that, there's Japs here, we can't do that."

At this point the Sgt with them yanked back the bolt on his Thompson submachine gun and threatened to shoot them if they didn't get up and get the trucks moving. They continued their protests while the Jap continued to plook the odd bullet into the soupy mud. "It wasn't their fault. This is what happens when you tell men they're incapable of fighting, they'll believe you. But now we had to carry the stuff back ourselves. So we each took 2 jerry cans of water and a box of K-Rations on our packs and slopped the two miles back. We didn't even kill the Jap, we just left him there and left them in the ditch."

They made it back sometime after dark. A few days later he spent his 22nd birthday, May 31st, in the muddy ruins of Dakashi town, waiting for orders to move up.

Scouts up! Advance to Itoman

While the 7th was rebuilding as best they could in the mud, the 5th Marines had taken Shuri Castle and the surrounding heights. At this point the main body of Japanese pulled back to make their final stand on the southern tip of the island. On June 2nd the 7th moved out as part of the general advance, getting orders to cut across the Oruku Peninsula and reach the coast just above the town of Itoman, which they did on June 7th.

It was a swift advance by Okinawa standards and the 7th covered 10,000 yards over the following week. This stretched the supply lines and on a number of occasion's ammo, food and water were dropped to the assault battalions by air. The going was not without hazards, however, as the Japanese had left rear guard elements all across the Peninsula to delay the advance. The terrain was gullied and still had plenty of vegetation as it hadn't been shelled into a moonscape. The scouts were called upon frequently to probe ahead and find crossings of streams, recon small settlements and, well, be scouts.

During this time he and another guy were probing ahead across a small stream on a rickety bridge. Just as he was moving across a Nambu machine gun opened up on them, striking the heel of his boot and clipping it off. "It knocked me ass over band box but I got up and kept running. You never see two men run so fast," he told me.

On another occasion they were moving through a fairly untouched settlement. "Outside one of the homes there was this fat Jap scowling at us. He had this big goldfish pond. I wasn't in any mood for his shit so I walked up and flipped a grenade into it. He started yelling and jumping around until one of the gunnys drew up on him with a Thompson and that ended that. He got right the hell out of there and left us the hell alone."

One evening during this drive they were in their night positions and heard a commotion coming towards them on the road. Thinking it was some kind of Banzai attack they opened fire. They were promptly mortared for most of the night. Dawn revealed piles of dead Okinawan civilians, driven down the road at bayonet point so the Japanese could locate the Marine line. Dad's feelings against the Japanese were hardened further.

And so it went, patrol, advance, scout, eliminate a pocket of Japs, advance again. He related to me how the machine guns firing cover when they would return from a scout would knock out "Shave and a haircut, two bits" in chorus.

A day or so later the 7th had reached the coast and was poised above Itoman town for the next big push south onto Kunushi Ridge, where the Japanese were preparing their last stand.

Itoman Town

On June 10th the 7th assaulted south towards Kunushi, crossing the Mukue Gawa, into Itoman town. Resistance stiffened and the fight through town became intense. 5 officers were lost in seven minutes.

June 10th saw the 2nd Battalion moving into northern Itoman. Having reached the sea, the Marines were able to utilize LVT Amtracs, which were used to shell and machine gun the town from the beach side. The battalion commander moved his command post to an LVT and had his artillery liaison officer with him. From the LVT moving along out at sea 100 to 200yds, and forward of his lines, the battalion commander was able to gain better observation of his assault units and the terrain they were negotiating than he could on shore. They called in everything they could onto the defenders. "They threw lots of naval guns onto it, but the battleship 16 inchers were impressive. They sounded like boxcars flying overhead and when they hit they threw you off the ground," Dad recalled.

Itoman was defended heavily. In moving through it, the 2nd Battalion, as mentioned, lost five officers in approximately seven minutes. This is probably where his platoon lieutenant William "Tiny" Myers was hit. He recalled that they were terribly upset by this. Myers was a tall man who went out of his way to take care of his people and his wounding filled them with a deep rage. Sometime that evening they heard Japanese soldiers singing and cheering and generally carrying on in what sounded like a big booze up. The next moring they charged. "They got all of 50 yards before they started to fall out, having been up all night and drunk," he said. "We waited until they got close and cut 'em up. That was my "Banzai" charge. It seemed a terrible waste."

After occupying the town, caves had to be destroyed and mines in the streets removed. Patrolling toward Kunishi and Mezado was attempted, resulting in several casualties from the intense enemy fire. Supply and evacuation were carried out by using the amphibious tractors, with the wounded going straight to the hospital ships off shore.

During this time a patrol from Fox Company got cut off in part of town near the coast and he and some other scouts were sent to find them and bring them back. They did this, at no small risk, and brought them back to their lines along the sea wall. He reported that they were not terribly happy with the F Company guys and let them know it.

Cauldron at Kunushi Ridge.

On June 11th 2/7 pushed out of Itoman and became fully engaged in what would become the fight for Kunushi Ridge, one of the last major strongholds of Japanese on the island. It got mean, fast. The entire feature was honeycombed with holes and tunnels and the Japs were everywhere.

1st and 2nd Battalions had tried to push across a valley to the front of the ridge during daylight, guiding along a small road that led to the top. Fierce fire stopped them in their tracks and sent them back. Accurate 47mm anti-tank fire knocked out a number of tanks whose movement was restricted by rice paddies. That night they tried again and, the Japanese not expecting that, got onto the ridge. At daybreak, and for the next five days all hell broke loose as the japs made their last stand with everything they had.

Again, battleship fire from USS Idaho was brought to bear along with airstrikes of 20 to 30 planes and all the Marine mortar and artillery fire they could muster. Still the japs held and only the smallest advances could be made by burning out each position, one at a time while machine gun and sniper fire swept the feature like a blizzard. Again they resorted to airdrops for re-supply, but all too often they landed mere yards outside the thin Marine line and it was too dangerous to retrieve them.

The small valley approach to the ridge was just as bad, swept by machine gun, mortar, artillery and snipers. The only way to get wounded out or reinforcements up was in the belly of Sherman tanks. That's how dad made it onto Kunushi the day after the first companies had established their toe hold. He was one of 54 men to take this risky ride, six per tank.

"They put us in these things and buttoned 'em up. Told us when we got there we'd have to go out the hatch in the bottom because the fire was too intense and they had already lost some guys," he told me. "I had seen what had happened to the first few that had been knocked out. Their armor wouldn't even slow down a Jap 47 and I was scared shitless. The whole way across I could hear rounds pinging off the side. They dropped that hatch and I got the hell out of that thing as fast as I could and got as far away from it as I could. Tanks were handy, but they're a bullet magnet. I hated being near them."

He then spent the rest of the fight like everyone else, crawling through the muck like arts, hiding from shells, blasting at Japs and suspected Japs and praying like hell they didn't get killed. Again the Japanese fire was so intense and accurate the Marines couldn't risk trying to get to the dead and they laid where they fell. They could barely get the wounded out.

By the 17th they had fought through Kunushi and gained a hold on the next one, Mezado Ridge. By then 2nd Battalion was fought out with only 87 men left standing in Easy Company, out of a strength of around 247 men and 7 officers when they landed. The other companies had suffered horrendous loses as well, with F Company having 43 remaining, and George Company 45.

It was to be 2nd Battalion's last full action of the campaign. On the morning of the 17th they were relieved in place by 22nd Marines who with 8th Marines fought past Mezado and to the southern shore, where the remaining Japanese committed ritual suicide.

Until June 22nd, when organized hostilities were declared over, they remained around Kunushi and policed up their dead, buried the Japs where they were and smoked out the last few defenders. The 7th was then ordered into a zone of responsibility to mop up remaining Japanese forces and do their best to clean up the battlefield. This involved smoking out the remaining Jap survivors from their caves and spider holes with demolition charges and flame throwing tanks. It took into the first part of July for the island to be declared secure.

After their assigned areas were cleared, the 1st Marine Division moved back north to a "Rehabilitation" camp on the Motobo Peninsula, where it had all began. They were issued new clothes, weapons and gear if needed, and took on a large replacement draft filled with fresh kids (like dad had been a month and a half prior). They then started training in earnest for invasion of the main islands which everyone knew would be the last and terrible phase of the destruction of the Japanese Empire. They were told to expect 98% casualties on the beach. Years later dad was on a flight, seated next to a Marine returning home from Japan. They got to talking and the Marine related how he had toured the defenses around Tokyo Bay. By his estimation he didn't feel that anyone would have made it off the beach.

Then on August 6th and 9th the U.S. dropped the two atomic bombs on Japan and suddenly the war was over. The marines were stunned. "It was like they lifted a death sentence off our heads," he told me. "I saw veteran Marines of multiple campaigns break down and cry. People can say what they want, but I experienced how the Japanese fought. They had no regard for life. Everything revolved around dying with honor for the Emperor. We would have had to kill every one of them. You'll never convince me it was the wrong thing to do."

All told 1st Marine Division suffered 2,283 men killed in action, 12,619 wounded, 25 missing, 305 died of wounds. (which was probably higher, eventually, as casualties evacuated to the hospital ships went onto the hospital rolls and off the division's, thus only being counted by the division once, as "wounded.")

The Divisions original strength on L-Day was around 16,000 to include support personnel and special units attached. So with a combined total of 15,232 casualties the division suffered almost 100% losses for the campaign, with the line units kept going only by steady influx of replacement drafts. If anyone doubts the total commitment of the Japanese to defend to the death read those numbers again...

Dad also shared other memories that weren't necessarily tied to a particular event. I have related them here.

Kickapoo Joy Juice

They would steal a jeep or cannibalize a destroyed one for their gas tanks. They would wash out the remaining petrol with sea water and then everyone would pool their canned fruit rations together, putting them all into the tank with fresh water and yeast they would barter the cooks for. In the pacific sun it of course fermented nicely and they would strain it out through t-shirts and get lit on the stuff. Occasionally the mixture was a bit too rich, the cap to tight and the tank vent would fail. "We'd be sitting there and all of a sudden one of them would explode, blasting straight up into the air as we all dove for cover thinking it was a shell. The stuff tasted horrible but it did the trick."

"Red" the sniper

"We had this sniper. He was a kid from Alabama and he had red hair so of course that's what we called him. He couldn't read. The Marine Corps had to teach him how to spell his name so he could sign his checks and his GI insurance forms. He had this 30-06 Springfield with this big, long scope on it. You could read a newspaper at 100 yards with it. He'd slide out in front of our line at dusk or before sunrise and get set up. And then we'd hear, BAM! We'd yell out, 'You get him Red?' and he'd call back, 'Ah got him.' I don't know to this day how many Japs he killed. Came through it without a scratch, never got hit, not once."

Pass the BAR

He related that the BAR, or Browning Automatic Rifle, was much favored in the line companies. Everyone was trained to use it so if they were in a bind, pinned down by Japs in caves or holes, they would just hand it down the line to whoever could get a bead on them. "It was heavy, so you could control it. You could empty a 20 round clip in about 3 seconds."

Mud Guns

The Reising submachine gun was a well enough made weapon. Easier to manufacture and lighter than a Thompson the Marine Corps had purchased thousands of them. There was a design flaw, however, that allowed mud to get into the back of the receiver, causing it to jam. Unacceptable in a combat weapon. He said that whenever they got them they would stomp them down into the mud and claim it as a battlefield loss and swap out for a Thompson or a carbine. "God knows how many thousands of them are still buried out there," he related.

A Jap "Knee Mortar" is not a "Knee" mortar

The Japanese fielded a small, hand held mortar in 50mm known as a Type 89. It fired more like a grenade launcher than what western armies would think of in a mortar and the Japs were very good with them, able to put out lots of fire, accurately. It did not have bi-pod legs like a U.S. 60mm mortar. They just held it at a 45 degree angle and tripped the trigger bar. The baseplate was curved, intended to be placed on a log. No matter how many times the word went out that it was not intended to be placed on the leg, there was always someone who had to try. In dad's case it was a replacement who found one when they were pushing down to Itoman. Before anyone could stop him he tried it and was soon on his way to the rear with a broken femur. "You could hear them 'Pop' when they fired them. You had a few seconds to get cover. They were small but they fired lots of them and they had a pretty good blast."

Spam is Banned

So I went to this youth leader camping thing once when I was in the 7th grade. (Camp Chewonki I think?) Well, for breakfast we had Spam cooked on the griddle. I came home all enthusiastic about this and wanted us to get some. Flatly and ruthlessly veto'd. Period. No Spam would ever be allowed in the home. Ever. "Half the time that's all we got. You couldn't make a fire because they'd hammer you with artillery so we ate it cold. The sight of it makes me sick." That was forty years after the fact.

Jungle Rot and Malaria

The Marines throughout the pacific Campaign were plagued by a condition commonly referred to as "Jungle rot." The technical term is "Tropical Ulcers." They are often initiated by minor trauma, and subjects with poor nutrition are at higher risk. That pretty much sums up the average Marine on campaign...a million ways to open the skin, living on field rations, and perpetually exhausted. Prime candidates. He told me that he wore his canvas leggings under his dungarees but it was no use, especially on an island as biologically contaminated as Okinawa was. His case went down to the bone. They had some kind of blue ointment they tried on it but it didn't really work. You could still see the scars on his legs right up until he passed away.

At some point he caught malaria. Not sure if he caught it on Okinawa or coastal China but he had recurrent bouts of it right into the 1950s.

MacArthur: No Love Lost

He was not fond of MacArthur. This was not uncommon of Marines. The feeling was that while the Marines had island hopped time and again, the US Army had gotten to lead in the final victory, being the force that occupied Japan itself. "He didn't care about us," was what he said. I'm sure that what happened on Peleliu, the destruction of the 1st MARDIV for an airfield that was never used, weighed heavily on all of them and influenced this thinking.

Seabees

He spoke very highly of the Seabees. (145th Naval Construction Battalion was the unit attached to 1st MARDIV.) During the campaign they performed herculean tasks to open and keep roads open, even during the terrible deluge of May. Because of this the Marines were rarely short of heavy artillery support and the big gun battalions were able to follow the line units as they fought their way down the island. He particularly remembered the camps they built for them on Motobo after the fighting had ended and how quickly they were able to build airfields.

A Catholic Chaplain

Mother Madge died while Dad is on Okinawa. A USMC Catholic chaplain was helpful during this time, as he recalled to my sister. One cannot imagine how overwhelming that must have been to be informed of that news when in the middle of that horror show. The speed of communication at the time would have meant that her funeral would have been long over by the time word got to dad.

Net Pay Scale

For this entire ordeal he was paid a base rate of $56.70 a month as a Marine PFC. At least he didn't pay income tax and the cigarettes were free.

Last of the China Marines

After the surrender of the Japanese on September 2nd, 1945 there were still a lot of loose ends to be tied up in the Pacific theater. Among them were 630,000 Japanese troops still in mainland china around Peking and the northern provinces. Being the only real force left standing, the job of securing and repatriating them fell to the Marines of the 3rd Amphibious Corps, to include 7th Marines. Thus began Operation Beleaguer, the U.S. occupation of Hopeh and Shantung Provinces, mainland China.

Given the mission of demobilizing the Japanese, returning Chinese nationalist forces of Chiang Kai Shek to previously Japanese held areas, and protecting the international legations. The Marines found themselves in an exotic land, in the middle of a civil war between the Nationalists and the Communists under Mao Ze Dong. By the end of October all major 1st Marine Division units were ashore.

Dad's memories of China were for the most part positive and he told them freely. It was a pretty exotic place for a 22 year old kid from Brunswick, Maine. As the Marines were the supreme force in the land, except for some minor problems with Communist guerillas, they pretty much owned the place. It was not a particularly dangerous post, you could relax. There is a picture of dad in his dress uniform in a rickshaw on the streets of Shanghai. Nothing of that sort ever happened on Okinawa.

The Shanghai to Tientsin Railroad

A large part of 2/7's mission was to guard the coal trains that ran from the mines around Tientsin down to the coaling stations of Shanghai harbor. He recalled that as they would leave the stations the Chinese would swarm onto the trains and just as quickly the Marines would go car to car kicking them off. In some cases literally throwing them bodily off the cars. They had their orders and that was that. It was probably for the best as the train runs were rarely free from incident as the war between Mao's Communists and Chiang Kai-Shek was starting to heat up now that the Japanese were gone.

A pretty regular occurrence was destruction of bridges or the tearing up of rails. A common trick was for the Communists to pull the spikes on one of the rails and leave it in place. The engineers wouldn't see it and the engine would derail, necessitating the repair crews each train carried to jump down and fix it. "These Chinese engineers were crazy. Half the time we didn't know if they were Communists or what. They'd run at night and just open it wide open and go as fast as they could. We'd bounce along in the back cars, hang on and pray they wouldn't hit anything."

Then one night they did. A coal train under Marine guard rear ended a train from the United Nations Relief and Rehabilitation Administration (UNRRA) carrying a load of flour from the United China Relief organization. The coal train was, of course, going at full speed. "We were running along and then all of a sudden you heard the most god awful crash. We were thrown ass over bandbox off the back and the whole train just jack knifed up into the air. The engineers were killed outright, scalded to death when the boiler blew. We looked around and the whole area looked like it had been hit by a snowstorm and we figured out pretty quick that it was flour from the box cars of the relief train. It didn't take long for nearby villages to come looking to see what had happened. They were all starving and they started scooping up handfuls of it from the ground and putting it in baskets. One of these Chiang Kai-shek officers came running down the tracks and tried to stop them. They were all corrupt and the whole load was probably headed for their officer's mess. We showed him the business ends of our M1s and sent him packing. From there on we started unloading 50lb bags onto anyone who could carry them. By morning word had spread and you could see the torches snaking down through the hills as people came in from the villages. We probably did more to aid those people in one night than the UN did the whole time they were there. "

On other occasions the Chinese engineers were communist infiltrators and they'd dump the coal hoppers onto bridges in an attempt to burn them. "We'd be on the back watching the flames climb higher and higher as we'd roll by. Between that and them prying up a rail, we'd get stuck out there. They'd tell us that a run down to Shanghai was a two day trip. They'd give us a box of K rations and a 2 quart can of grapefruit juice. Well, we'd get stranded for four or five days at a time out there while they fixed it all. The Communists would harass the repair crews by sniping at them and slow things down. There were these grave mounds scattered across all the fields. They'd tuck down in there and pop shots off at us. They couldn't hit a bull in the ass with a shovel but they scared the hell out of the coolies. You could never really see them so we really didn't bother to shoot back. So there we'd sit, running out of rations and drinking grapefruit juice."

Village Life

On other occasions they'd be detailed out into the villages on mapping missions. On one occasion they were rolling through one in their jeeps and a Chinese man dashed out and threw a bundle under the lead jeep. "We thought it was some kind of bomb but it didn't go off. We looked and turns out it was a baby girl. The Chinese didn't have much use for girls and they would leave them out in the hills to die. Well, this guy comes up and starts demanding money for the kid because we had killed it. The sergeant with us listened to this for a bit and then unloaded his Thompson on him. We never had that problem again."

On another occasion they were billeted above the town in an old mission school. They really didn't give a damn about these missions so they would brew jungle juice and get drunk. One of the guys from the machine gun section got so high on it that he belted up the .30 cal and proceeded to blast the hell out of the place from the inside. Dad bailed and walked down to the village, about half lit himself. When he got there he saw all these Mongolian ponies tied up on hitching rails. Being the horseman that he was he helped himself to one of them and proceeded to trick ride the thing, American style, up and down the street.

Turns out the ponies belonged to a Mongolian bandit group that were taking advantage of the Chinese instability to do what Mongolian bandits did, raid and loot Chinese towns.

"They were tearing up the place pretty good but they saw me on their pony and they all came out to watch the little Marine do cowboy tricks. They were pretty impressed by this and showed me a few of their own. About then our captain came wandering in. He talked to the leader and explained that in a sense the town was under our protection and these guys tearing it up would make us loose face. He didn't want a fight with them, but business was business. The bandit leader said that if he let the little Marine come down and show them "Indian" tricks they'd stop molesting the people. He agreed and so I'd go down there over the next few days and we'd trick ride and feast. After a few days they refitted and rode on."

Shanghai: Adventure City

Shanghai was one of China's most cosmopolitan cities. For a hundred years or so there had been a sizeable foreign legation in the city tied to its position as a gateway for maritime trade with the world. Silk, spice and opium were major export items. It was colorful, chaotic, and a melting pot of ancient china and the world. The Grand Monde, one of the main centers of entertainment, hosted a panoply of distractions; theater, cafés, restaurants, gaming rooms, and cinema, which surprisingly bounced back fairly quickly despite the savage Japanese occupation and civil war. It must be noted that Marines were paid in hard currency. For those granted leave or a pass there they were as flush as kings.

At some point during one of these leaves, dad was in some kind of bar with his fellows. Drink flowed as it did amongst the combat veterans of the Corps. As he related, there were a number of Chinese Nationalist officers in the establishment. These officers were noted for their corruption and their total lack of caring for either the people or their own men. They were universally loathed by the Marines.

"So we were in there and this one officer kept eye balling me. Normally I wouldn't have cared but he had this nice pair of Mauser pistols with silver inlay and ivory grips and we hated them anyway. I got sick of him and decided to get into a fight. We got into it and I wound up throwing him out of the second floor window. I jumped into the street after him and whipped his ass some more. That's how I got those pistols." Years later my mother left them unsecured in the house and they were stolen by contractors.

The Paris Market in Shanghai had long been a hub of trade, funneling in the fineries of China for centuries. For a young Marine flush with hard currency it was an exciting place. Some of the items he purchased included a silver pocket watch featuring a Chinese Dragon with small rubies for eyes. He also obtained some other silver pieces. One big purchase he made was 20 yards of the finest silk he could find, for 19 cents a yard. He bundled it up and sent it to Nana, who I guess was known to the family (Gramp married her in 1948, so she must have been in the mix somehow). When he got home she thanked him profusely and asked why he didn't send more, as the same silk in America at the time was largely unobtainable or prohibitively priced. She had never written back. Typical Maine mindset, I hate to say, where so much goes unspoken.

A darker side of China, however, was the utter disregard for individual life. Public executions were an everyday occurrence and his scrap album had many pictures of them. Not sure if he took these or purchased them. It's not surprising that these things would fascinate the combat veterans of the Pacific, being so alien to American thinking. He remarked on a number of occasions how Asia didn't have much respect for human life.

Coming Home

In March of 1946 he was shipped home from China and mustered out of the USMC at Bainbridge, MD on the 4th of April. His rotation home was most likely due to the combat points earned on Okinawa and the backfill of late war enlistees and replacement drafts that were already in the pipeline. His travel allowance from Maryland to Portland was $24.95, on top of a mustering out pay of $217.17.

He apparently neglected to write, telegram or call anyone. He just showed up on the doorstep. Typical Mainer but not an uncommon story for returning veterans who most likely spent the long trip home reflecting and decompressing from what they had been through.

Post War Michigan State

Like many veterans dad returned to finish school at Michigan State. The dean was a WW1 guy, he knew what was going to be up with all these returning combat vets. He put all those guys in housing together and had them take basket weaving classes for the first year. Wise move on his part as this was the age before an understanding of PTSD or other issues returning veterans face. There wasn't a whole lot of "re-integration" programs. The thing those guys got was a stiff drink and a "carry on." An entire generation had to pretty much grope their way through coming back from such a life transforming event as best they could. As Sid Phillips said in the The Pacific, "You get up and get on with your day, and after a while you forget some things."

Sometime in the fall of '46 dad joined the SAE fraternity. They had their frat house and it was by all accounts a lively place, filled with veterans in full "unwinding." On one occasion they had a Hawaii themed party and constructed a large pool in front of the place. To get in you had to cross a gangplank of sorts. As was many times the case the campus authorities arrived and tried to calm things down. The vets holed up on the balcony and challenged them to enter the place. They all fell into the pond and that put an end to the incursions. That and the dean of students probably put the word out to leave them alone.

In the next couple of years dad settled back into the routine of finishing vet school. They were lean times. He had moved past the frat house and was camping in the vet clinic on a cot in a small room in the back. At one point they got the call that a farmers cow had died. They went out and sure enough, there was a dead cow. They told the farmer that they needed to take it back to the clinic for an "autopsy" to determine the cause of death. I don't recall if they ever determined cause, but they devoured the thing over the next week.

Post-Graduation

Upon graduation he returned to Maine and to Naples where Gramp had the stables. In a short time they built a small building where he would establish a local, small animal practice. This was to be short lived. I remember the slab where it had stood was still there.

"The animals were fine, it was the owners that drove me out," he recalled. "I really didn't have the patience for it." An early indication that post-Pacific War sensibilities were going to be an issue came from "Fifi" the yappy dog. "I was like, 'There, there, be nice' and it bit me. I tried a second time, and it bit me again. The third time I backhanded it off the table. Its owner scooped it up and rushed out. I never did see her again." That was followed by a cat that got away as he was trying to neuter it. "It went way up into this tree. I tried to call it, I put out food, but it wouldn't come down. By the third day I was furious so I got out the .30-30 and brought him down. I told them it died under anesthesia and charged them $5 to bury it. That was the end of small animal work." War makes you short tempered.

Years later, when he and Mom Betty were in Cuba a friend had a pet monkey that was sick so he agreed to take a look at it. It bit him on the thumb, and he bore the scar for the rest of his life. The reason the monkey was sick was because it had rabies. That was followed by the old school rabies treatment of 23 shots in the stomach. Yea, small animal work was just bad juju all around.

Now I understand that the whole cat thing is probably horrifying and if one didn't know him closely they might think he was some kind of monster. That wasn't the case. He was maybe only 4 or five years out of the war at that time. Tempers were short in those days. This was the same guy who went out to hunt one fall and had a deer walk up to him while he was sitting on a stump. He had it dead to rights, but instead of shooting looked at it thought, "What a beautiful thing," and let it walk off.

He never really hunted again until I came of age and only then because, "You have to know how to put food on the table." Even then, except for duck hunting, it was a halfhearted effort. I never really did become a deer hunter, ask my brother. He still razz's me about the time I built a campfire one cold, deer hunting morning. I just didn't care. There was a brief "Mountain Man" phase which had me hunting squirrels and such. But I left one in back of the barn once and Dad went up one side of me and down the other for wasting its life. That was really the end of the hunting phase.

This was also the guy who wouldn't close the barn doors from May through September because the barn swallows would come back from the south and nest in the rafters. This was the guy that got me a birdcage and provided syringes so I could hand raise the chicks that had fallen out of the nests. For a guy who didn't want to work on small animals, the place in New Gloucester was Noah's Ark. At the height of it we had; two dogs, five cats, an old thoroughbred from the track, two ponies, two cows, six sheep, nine geese, 48 ducks, and god knows how many other animals lurking around in the wood lot. This was the guy who let me bring home a wild duck I had captured in the reeds on a duck hunting trip to Meremeeting Bay. I was out looking for a duck that I had shot and there was a mallard drake that had hunkered down. I chased him through the mud flat until I tackled him. I brought it back to the boat and we stuffed it into one of the decoy bags. Dad built a pen for it and I tried to tame it, which of course was a failure. Eventually he broke it to me that I wasn't going to turn it into a pet so I took it down to the river and released it. These kind of stories are a regular staple of my childhood.

More Post War Stories

The Korean War broke out in the spring of 1950 and the South Koreans and their American "advisors" got their asses handed to them. It was a pitiable route but reinforcements from Japan arrived and the army was able to hold onto a bridgehead around the southern city of Pusan. As the war turned into a United Nations, American led, crusade against communism there was lots of talk about recalling WW2 vets who were still listed on the rolls of the inactive reserve. This did not sit well. "We were sweating that one. We knew what it was all about. I did one war. I wanted no part of another one," he said.

From The Copa Cabana to Tampa

Then there was the Cuba expedition. Before Castro, Cuba was a troubled but pretty happening place. He went down there with Betty, his first and third wife (long story) and started working on the horse track in Havana. These were a couple of years of real Hemingway stuff. Deep sea fishing, scuba and all kinds of things. Lots of vets went down there. It was the heyday of the casinos and the Copa Cabana. But then the revolution blew through and some fighting broke out in the neighborhood. This prompted dad and his veteran buddies to climb onto the roof, full of Mimosas, and cheer on the combatants. Betty put a stop to that, as she had a newborn and two dogs. She reeled him down and they took the boat to Tampa, tossing the keys to the house and the car to their gardener as they left. He worked the track, Florida Downs, pretty much till he passed away in '91.

Once they got to Florida, they lived in a trailer that was under the final approach to the Tampa airport. Dad remembered there was a set of cabinets above the headboard of the bed. They'd be sleeping and a plane would come in, he would bolt straight up in bed out of a dead sleep, and smash his head on them. They sounded like Jap artillery coming in. This was in the late 50s, early 60s. It only stopped when they moved over to McMullin Booth Road. We know today that that was what we now call PTSD. He never told me of any nightmares, but I'm sure they were part of it.

Later Years

He was never a "Gung Ho" Marine vet. It was a quieter expression, with a few books, probably Christmas gifts, on the bookshelf in the living room. There was also a box of post-war "Leatherneck" magazines in the attic. I still have them. He told me these things sometimes because he was angry with me. I was a dumb kid, running my mouth, and he would say, "No, you don't know. Let me tell you something..." I knew it was time to shut up and listen. That's when he relayed the stories of the real war. China was different. He enjoyed it there and told those stories easily. But the war stuff...you had to piss him off. He said, "It was a waste of good lives. I think about all the doctors, lawyers, engineers, all the young men who never got a chance at life because of it."

Around age 12 or so I asked the dumb shit question that most sons ask their veteran fathers, "Did you kill anyone." He paused for a moment, and replied, "I don't know. But I sure shot at a bunch of them though."

In the later part of the 1980s he joined the First Marine Division Association and received the newsletter. He was looking for LT Bill "Tiny" Myers in the rolls but never did find him. I've always kept my ears and eyes open for LT Myers but have never been able to locate him, even in the internet age.

Dad was quiet and not confrontational. If you pissed him off he would just sort of disappear you from his life. He'd seen real fighting. There was a couple notable times when he did get up in someone's grill, however, most notably the time in Florida when the KKK burned a cross down in what was called the "Colored Quarter" in those days. Most of the grooms on the track at the time were African American and when it started a couple of them came up the road and knocked on Dad's door. He was "Doc Bartlett" and, as a northerner, had always treated them with respect. He got in the car and went down there, shooing the Klansmen away. They made the mistake of repeating it a couple times and on the final affront he rode down there with an M1 carbine. "I told 'em that this wasn't going to happen ever again. 'What did these people ever do to you?' I asked them. I also dropped word into a few key ears that if certain people wanted a horse to ever start on that racetrack ever again this shit was going to stop." He's the track vet. He can scratch a horse from any race for any reason. The Klan never rallied in that neighborhood ever again. He wasn't necessarily an activist liberal, but he had that sense of simple justice and fairness. It's a story I'm pretty proud of.

If you look at the photos of him before the war there is a mischievous grin, a twinkle in his eye, bit of a rebel and a prankster who liked a good laugh. After the war it is gone. Replaced by a grim, steeled aspect that comes from the worst realities inflicted on a young soul. The only photo I know of him from that immediate after war time where he is smiling, genuinely happy, is the mug shot they made for him to get a license to buy liquor in Michigan that he got when he went back to school.

I'm pretty sure I was there the day the war finally ended for him. Like I said before, the war wasn't a "front and center" feature of his life. It was there in the background, something terrible that had shaped him in his youth. It would come out in small ways like no spam in the house, no Japanese products (until the Massey blew up and we got a Kubota), American cars only. Small, unspoken but lingering prejudices that were shared by a lot of Pacific Veterans, unavoidable given the savagery they were exposed to.

There was this one moment, however, that I think threw the switch on it. My mom (Mom Judy) was living in DC and I was in school in Fredericksburg. It was 1987 or '88. Dad was making his annual drive down to Florida to work that winter's race meet. We all met up in the city and decided to go see the US Marine Corps Memorial. As we were walking across the parking lot there was another family a short distance away headed in the same direction; a young Japanese couple and their father. The older Japanese man and dad saw each other at about the same time and froze, their gazes locked. They knew. They just knew. The Japanese man bowed slightly, dad nodded in return. He said that we could go now. We got back to the car and he said, "He's about the same age as me. Nice looking family." And that was it. That was all he said. But you could feel something lifted off him, an unseen sigh, a breath held for so long released.

I'm pretty sure that that's the day the war ended and the last ghosts were laid to rest.

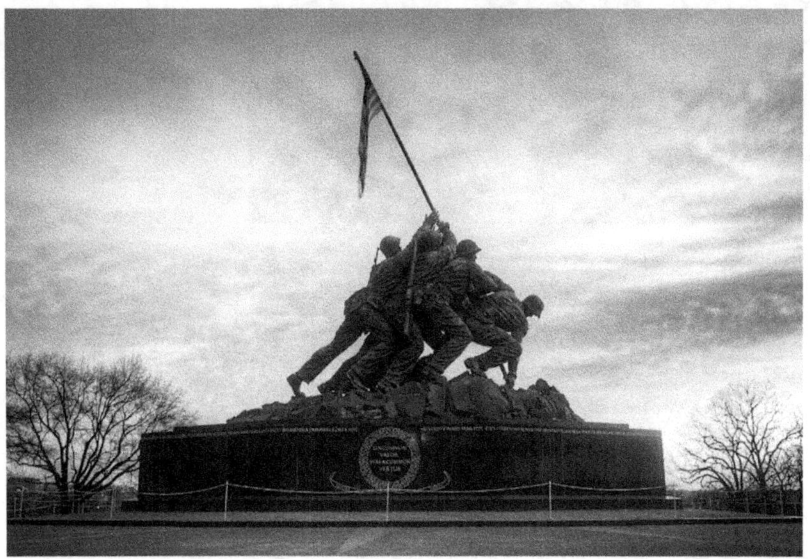

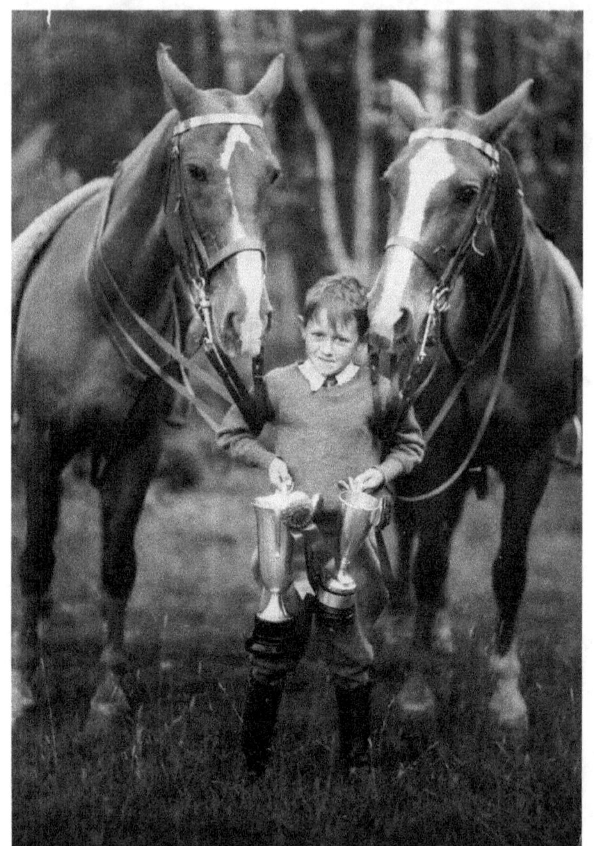

The son of a cowboy turned cavalryman, horses were a major part of Dad's life from the very beginning. One of our favorite photos of him is from a horse show in Brunswick sometime in the early 1930s. He already had a knack for bringing in the ribbons. They would remain the centerpiece of his life until the end.

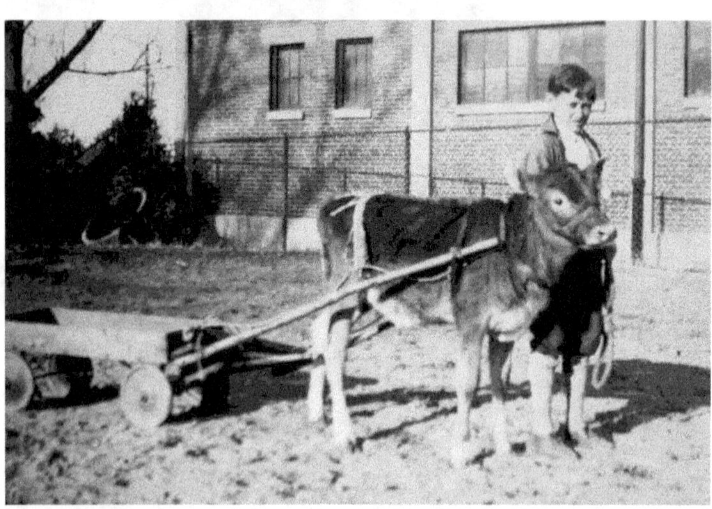

Pet calf in harness with the Red Flyer wagon contraption, circa 1935.

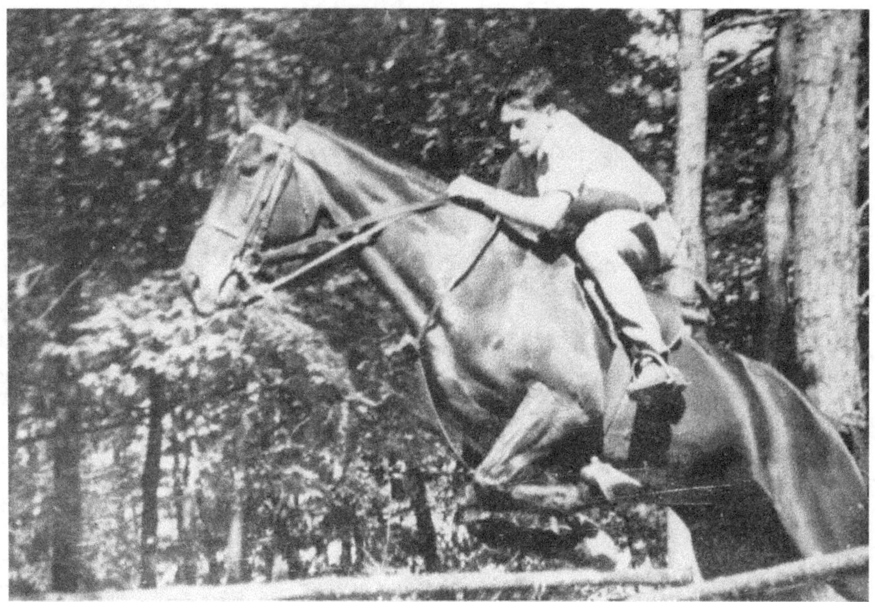

By his teen age years he was a consistent winner in the ring and was actively teaching horsemanship. It is little wonder he chose veterinary medicine and cavalry as his ROTC path in his college years.

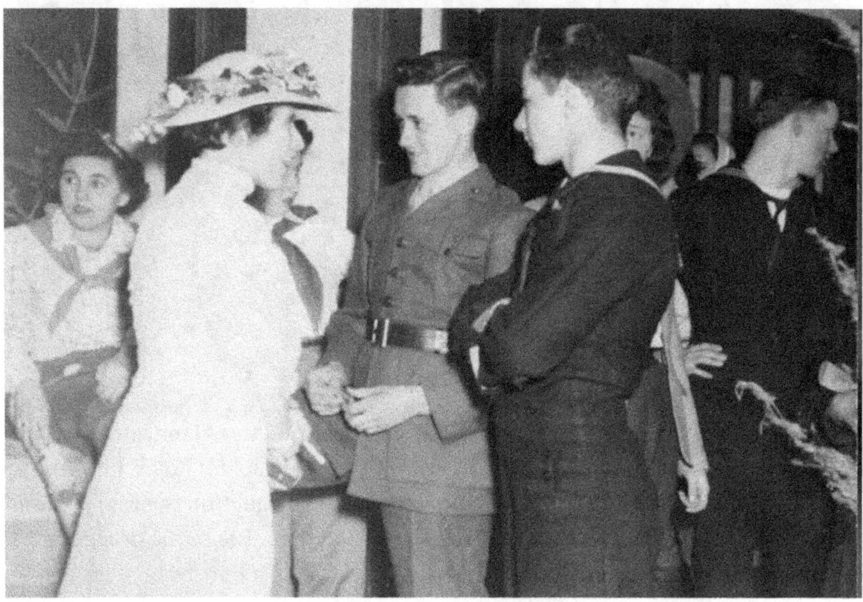

Christmas leave, 1944 in Brunswick shortly before shipping to California and then Okinawa. No ribbons, still smiling, but slightly harder.

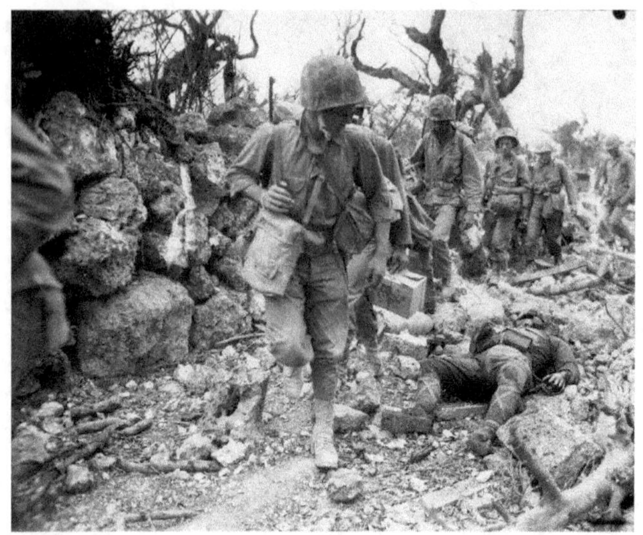

Marines passing by Japanese dead somewhere in the wreckage of Okinawa, 1945. As the battle dragged on the island became a massive open graveyard of unburied bodies, US and Jap alike. Flies and maggots covered nearly every surface in their vicinity.

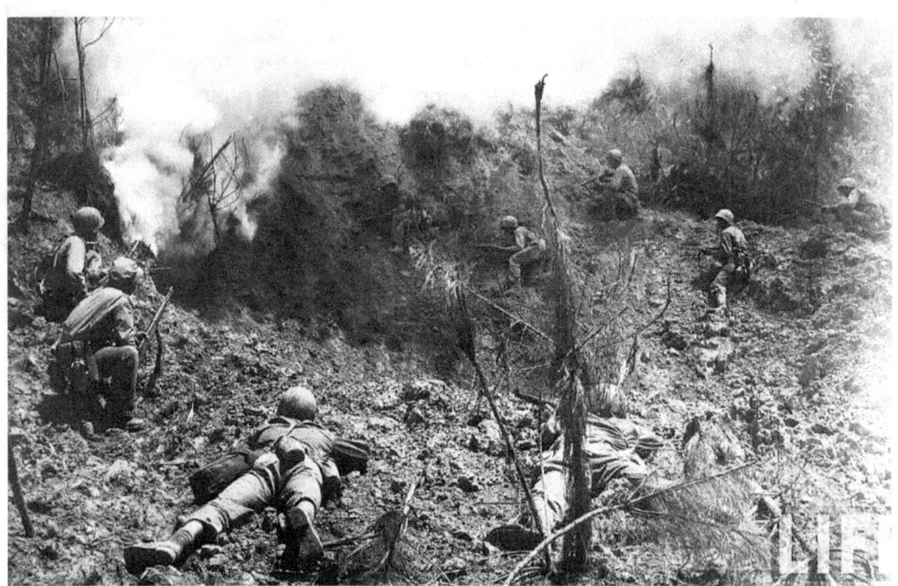

An army of 100,000 Japanese troops and conscripts met the Americans on Okinawa and sold their lives dearly. They had extensive tunnels, spider holes, bunkers, and every speck of ground zeroed with artillery. Into this cauldron the Marines went day after day, rooting them out of every cave and hole. The battle dragged on for 82 days and weeks thereafter of mop up. It foretold of a horrifying reception that awaited the Americans on the Japanese home islands, an invasion only avoided by the deployment of two atomic bombs.

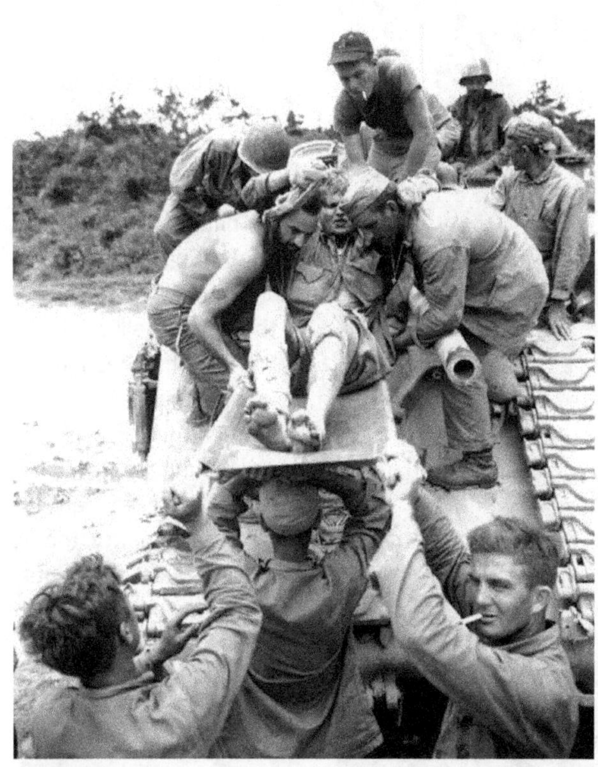

So intense was the fire before Kunushi Ridge that the Marines had to evacuate the wounded and ferry in replacements with tanks.

Massive naval, air, and land shelling reduced every town of note to rubble. Untold numbers of Okinawan civilians were caught in the crossfire and killed. Estimates run as high as 100,000.

In the middle of all this Dad turned 22 and was informed his mother had died.

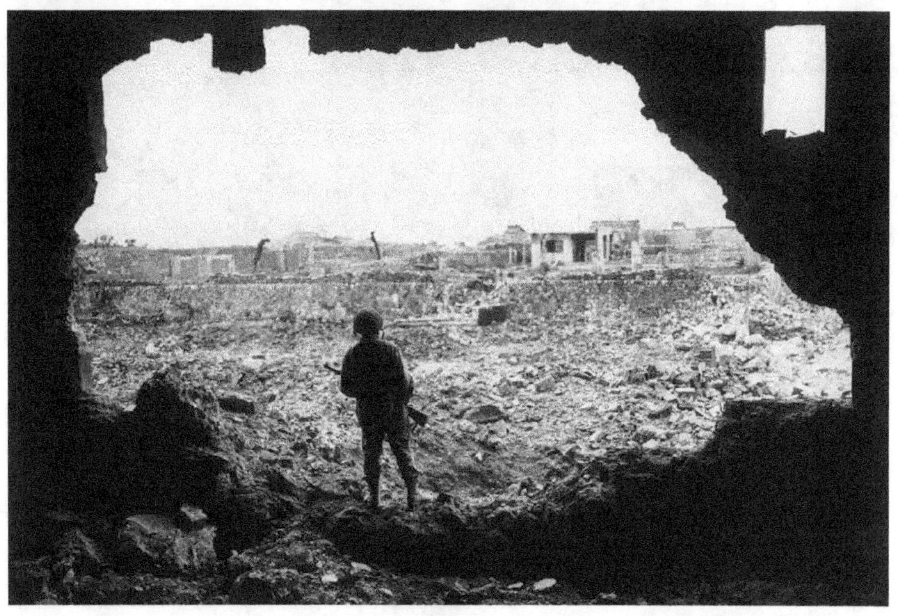

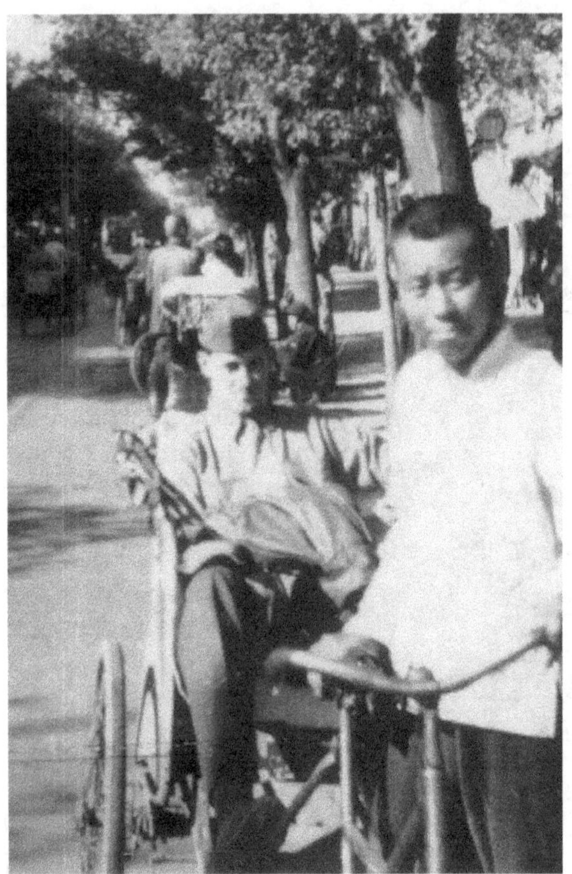

The last of the China Marines, 1946. Whether guarding coal trains from Tiensin, or taking leave in Shanghai, China was an exciting post for the 1st MARDIV. While not the deadly hellscape Okinawa had been, it was just dangerous enough to keep it interesting. Deployed across this exotic, and fractured country, the Marines were flush with cash and combat power. By all accounts they enjoyed themselves immensely.

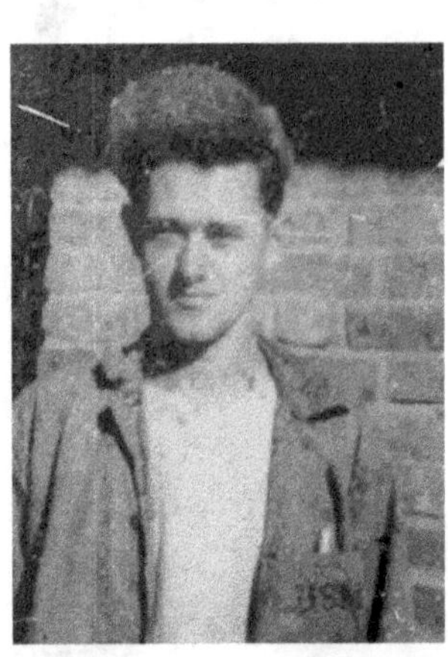

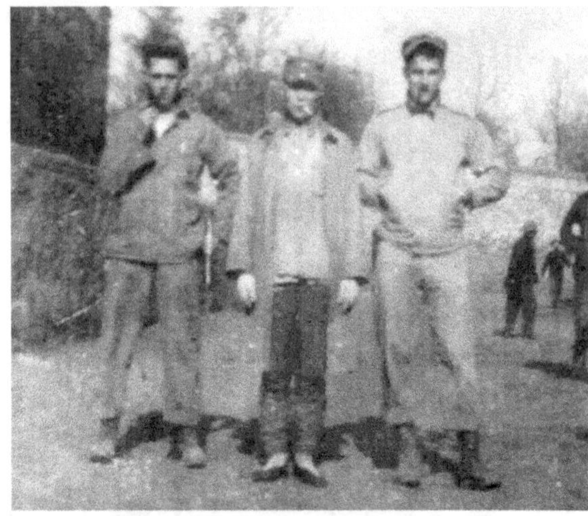

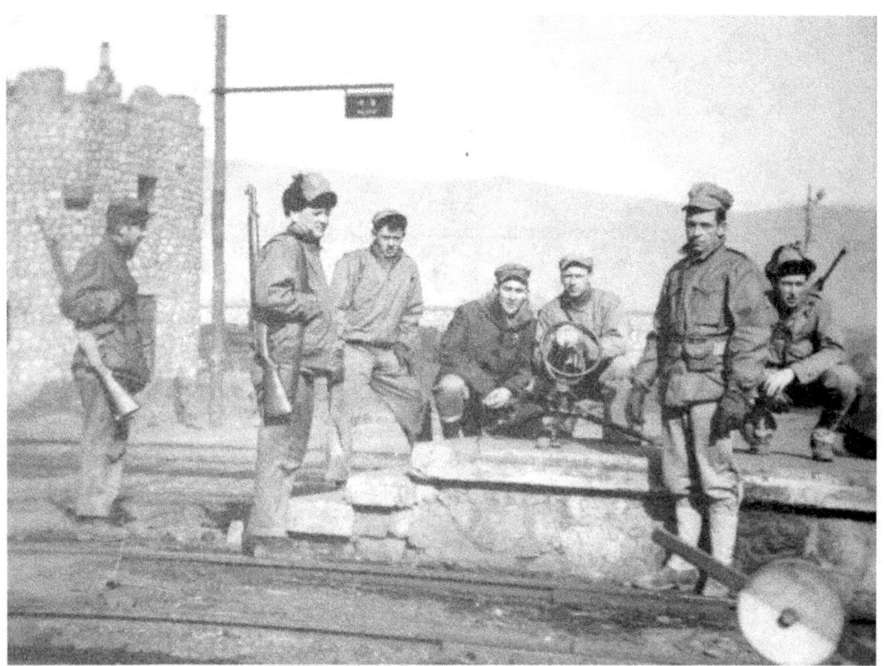

Waiting on a train. Rail siding somewhere in northern China. Dad 3rd from the left.

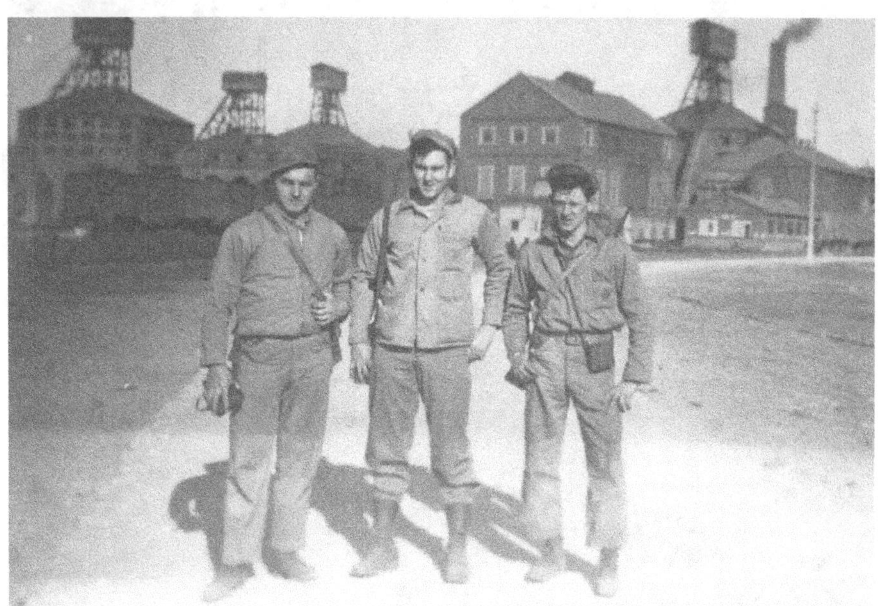

Coal mines at Tiensin China, 1946. For many months the Marines rode the trains that took it to the port city of Shanghai. (Dad on the right)

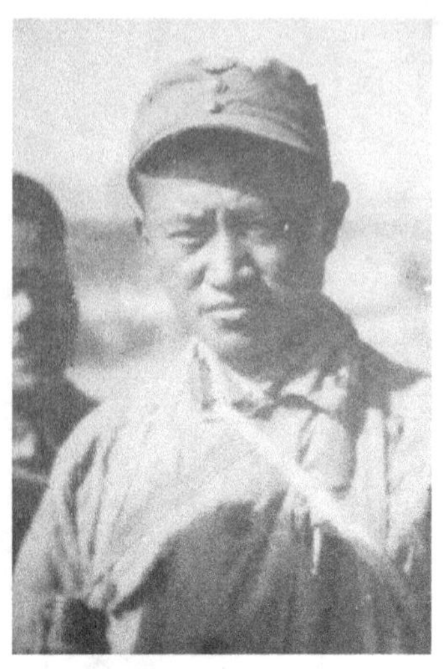

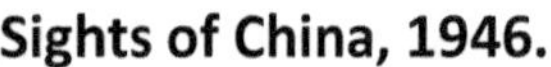

Sights of China, 1946.

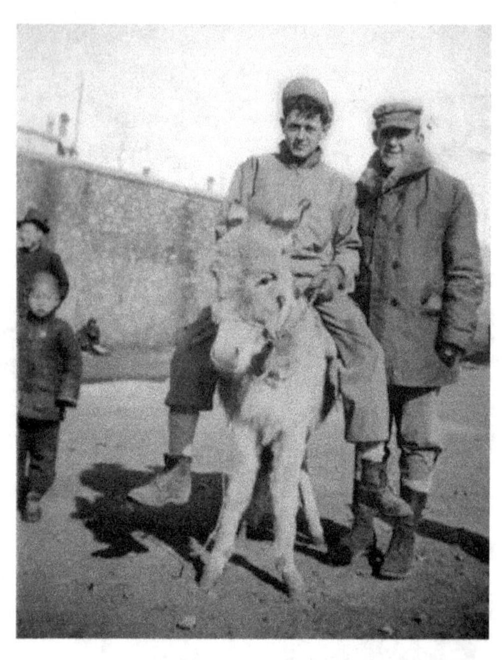

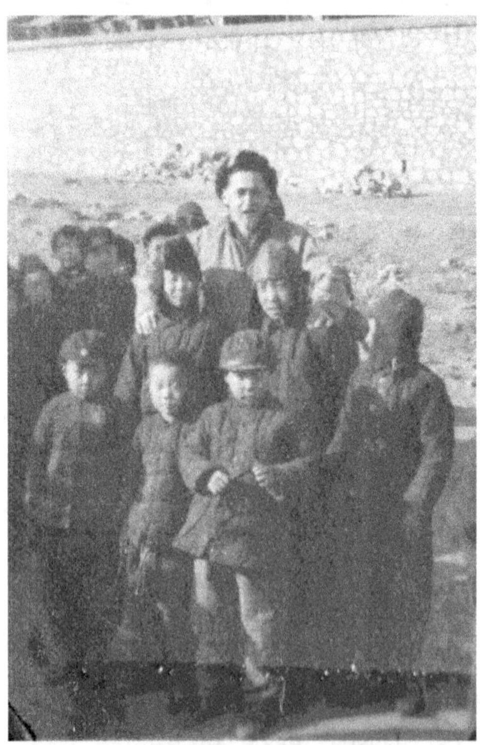

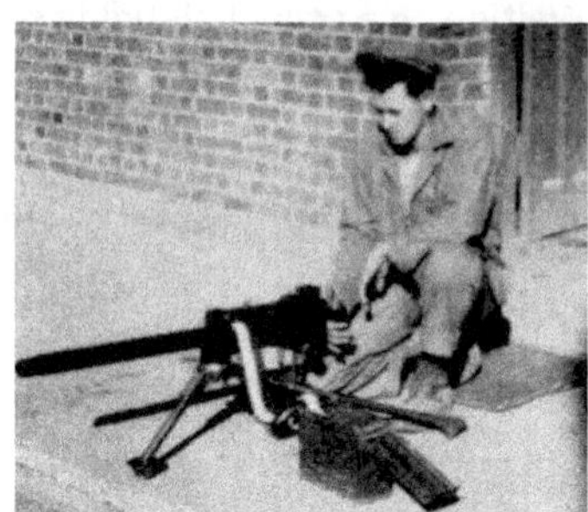

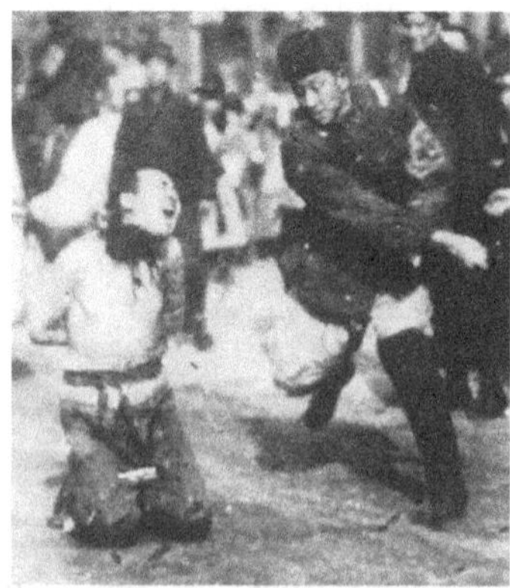

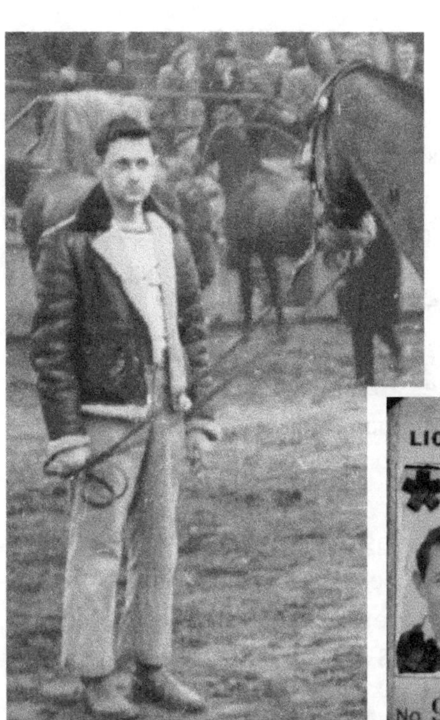

Older and hardened. Like many veterans the return home had its challenges. The sparkle of youth had faded, snuffed out by an unforgiving world. Happy day, however, on the day they issued the MI liquor license.

In later life he took great joy and comfort with the animals we kept.

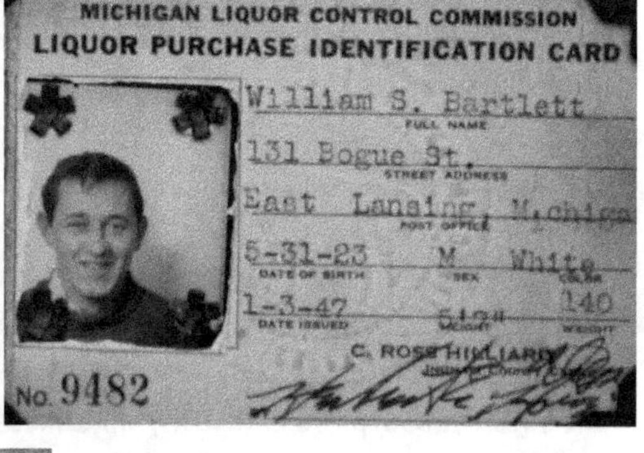

MICHIGAN LIQUOR CONTROL COMMISSION
LIQUOR PURCHASE IDENTIFICATION CARD

William S. Bartlett
FULL NAME
131 Bogue St.
STREET ADDRESS
East Lansing, Michiga
POST OFFICE
5-31-23 M White
DATE OF BIRTH SEX
1-3-47 [illegible] 140
DATE ISSUED
C. ROSS HILLIARD
No. 9482

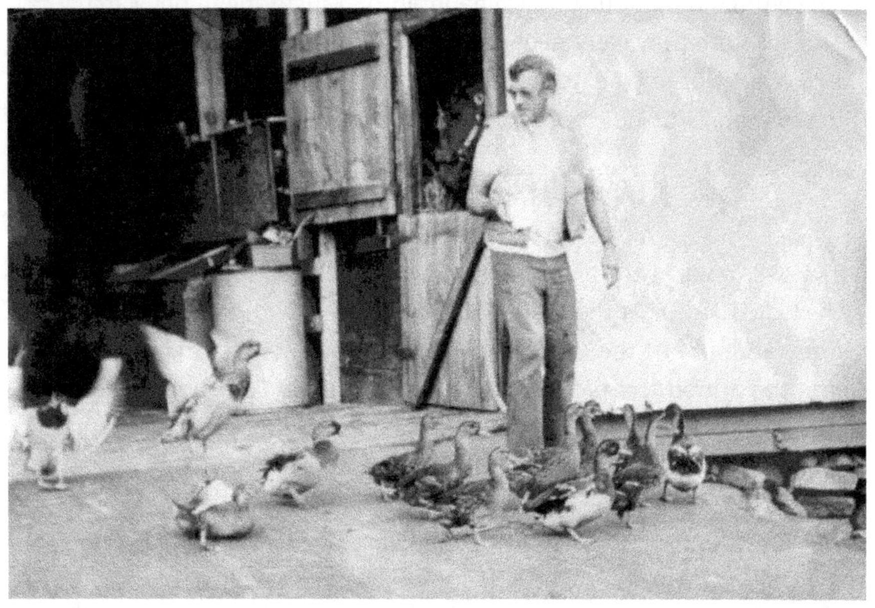

The Brooks Boys go to War 1917 - 1918

I come into the Brooks line via my step-mother Betty. Grandpa Hubert was her father and I came into some family stories of he and his brothers in The Great War; Raymond, Robert, and Paul. In 1917 President Woodrow Wilson had reversed his anti-war, isolationist stance and decided entry into the bloodbath in Europe was essential for the spread of democracy and Progressive ideals. All of the brothers, except for Charles (the oldest), enlisted for WW1 along with millions of other Americans in various capacities. No one who was swept up in the conflict, and the subsequent influenza pandemic of 1918, was ever the same again.

Official records are hard to come by as most of them burned in an archives fire in 1977 but between the family stories and surviving service cards I was able to piece together a great deal. Except for Robert, all the brothers served in the US Army Medical Department.

It's no real surprise that they all enlisted. Their father had been Capt. William Curtis Brooks (1826-1915) who served late in the Civil War.
He commanded K Co. 12th Maine Infantry, Mustering in on March 21st, 1865. Before they were even southbound Lee surrendered and the war was over. Not off the hook, however, they undertook occupation duty in Savanah, GA. They mustered out April 18, 1866.

US Army Medical Corps, 1917 - 1919

The U.S. underwent a massive, national mobilization upon entry into the war. The U.S. at the time was still operating with a minimal standing army and, like in the Civil War, hastily enlisted over a million civilians into the armed forces and many more into national support roles. The PBS series "The Great War" is an excellent documentary covering the scale of this. It involved the entire country.

Many of the infantry units we raised were thrown together en masse and shipped to France with little or no training. Some didn't even have rifles. The Army Medical Department, however, had their act together thanks to pioneering luminaries such as Col. Leonard Wood (of Yellow Fever fame) and the hard lessons of the Civil War, the Spanish American War, and the Philippine Insurrections. Thanks to Col. Johnathan Letterman of the Union Army, there was a foundation of the layered, military evacuation and hospital system in place. This survived the interwar years and was added to by scientific advancements in areas such as disease process, radiology, and aseptic surgical procedures. Antibiotics had yet to be invented, but these important advances saved the lives of countless wounded Doughboys in France.

In June of 1917 the Army established five primary medical training and mobilization camps; Camp Greenleaf, NC, Fort Oglethorpe, GA., Fort Riley, KS., Camp Crane, Allentown, PA., and Fort Benjamin Harrison, IN.

The days started early, 06:00 with revile, and ended at 21:30 when taps sounded. Officers and enlisted men had different courses of study but both averaged 180 hours of actual instruction and training a month. First there was the basics of military life; drill, manual of arms, military law, and other subjects necessary to turn civilians into soldiers.

Then there were the specialty trades of the Medical Department. The field hospitals and evacuation ambulance companies were taught proficiency in the school of the soldier, litter bearer drill, tent pitching and striking, individual cooking, transmission of messages, first aid, and the establishment and operation of hospitals and forward aid stations for the sick and wounded. Practice marches were also held. In addition, schools were conducted for instruction in operating-room technique, pharmacy, ward management and nursing, the administration of drugs, truck and ambulance driving, including the care of equipment and making repairs. The number of sub-schools established for various areas of medicine was bewildering and include all the modern specialties we know today.

SGT Hubert Weslie Brooks

57th and 60th Pioneer Infantry

Grandpa Hubert is not my blood relation, but come to me as step grandfather through momma Betty. I did, however, know him as a child and of course heard the family stories. He was a veteran of WW1 and by all accounts was a pretty cranky guy even before the war. One story I have been told was that his younger brothers would race home to the house from school and before he would arrive they would get inside and adjust all the window shades to differing lengths. This would drive him to fits and he would rush around fixing them all. He was never rude or mean to me in any way but his crankiness and being very particular was spoken of in hushed tones.

His service in "The Great War" was entirely stateside, he never shipped overseas as far as I can tell. He enlisted as a Private on July 3rd, 1917 with his brother, Paul, both reporting for duty on July 25th. He was assigned to the medical corps and spent most of 1917 and early 1918 training or working in the emerging camps on the east coast as America mobilized. He was initially assigned to the 57th Pioneer Infantry, which was built out from the 1st Infantry Vermont National Guard. In 1917 I believe they helped build out Camp Bartlett near Westfield, Mass as a mobilization center and then moved on to build Camp Greene near Charlotte, NC. There is a series of photographs showing the brothers in an Army camp. It was most likely here as their service took them down different paths after that.

In February 1918 the 57th moved on to Camp Wadsworth, near Spartanburg, SC. This camp had sprung up as one of the main mobilization points in the east and saw 10s of thousands men pass through. From there the 57th shipped for France on September 23rd 1918 through ports in New Jersey. I believe he stayed behind and continued to work the camp hospital at Wadsworth, as his service record indicates a reassignment to the 60th Pioneer Infantry, another unit that ran the SC post. He was de-mobilized on Dec. 27th, 1918 at Camp Devens, MA. As the 57th had shipped over and been broken up to backfill the frontline divisions in France during that period, the timeline is too tight for a trip to France and a stateside reassignment.

This was probably a good thing as the 57th was struck by Influenza as they departed their camp in New Jersey. On the passage over their troopship, the SS Leviathan, turned into a charnel house. Packed with 9,000 men the influenza ripped through it claiming almost 100 and desperately sickening nearly 1,000. That was one trip you didn't want to be on. The presence of 200 Army doctors and nurses on board saved them from worse.

During his year and a half of service he was promoted from Private to Sergeant, which is a pretty good run for a stateside billet. Probably had a lot to do with his being so particular and detail oriented. He didn't really tell me any stories, but knowing him is a personal connection with that era and I picked up details from my own studies later on.

I also remember an encounter with an old vet at the Gray Manor home for veterans where he lived when he was older. It was a big Victorian home in Gray, ME and I remember it had this big stone fireplace in the living room. On the mantle were several US and German helmets and other memorabilia. We would go to visit and momma Betty would take time to address whatever business needed doing with the staff while I would sit in the living room with these guys.

There was one encounter I shall never forget. He was a very big African-American gentleman and I was told he had been part of the Harlem Hellfighters. He started telling me a story about how one night they had gone out to raid a German trench. They had jumped down in there and got into close combat with the Germans. These kinds of trench raids were common, and brutal. He tells me how they snuck through their barbed wire and how they couldn't see them because they were black. As he's telling me this he's getting more and more agitated. "I jumped in on this one big bastard and grabbed him by the collar. I had me one of those trench knives and I smashed his face with it. Then I stuck it in his throat." By now he's right up in my face and he's grabbed me by my shirt. "I kept stabbing him and the blood gushed out all over my hand. It's still there, I can still feel it! Do you hear me, boy, it's still there!" By now he was very loud and the other men stepped in, ushering him away into another room. "All these years and it's still there," he mumbled as they led him away. I will never forget his eyes. God rest him wherever he is.

Pvt. Raymond Estes Brooks

303rd Field Hospital, AEF 1918

While I didn't hear much from Grandpa Hubert, one person I did hear spoken of was Hubert's brother Raymond Estes Brooks, who entered service on May 29th, 1918. He had made it to France, also in the medical corps. I was told that he had been gassed at some point and came home with shell shock. Aunt Anna had taken care of him in her home until he passed away some years later from pneumonia (1939, age 49). No doubt his lungs were compromised by the gas.

His first stop was the RCT 22nd Company, 6th Battalion, 159th Depot Brigade, a mobilization and training Camp Zachary Taylor, Indiana. I believe this was part of the Ft. Benjamin Harrison complex where they had a camp for initial medical training. Here he was issued the woolen greens and wrap around puttees that the doughboys wore and his days filled with initial training and drill. Living in these camps was cramped, with thousands of men under tentage. Sanitation was a bit better than it had been during the Civil War, which was the last time we mobilized on this scale, but not by much. Influenza would soon be tearing through these mobilization centers, killing thousands.

He was shortly pushed down to the 76th "Liberty Bell" Division towards the end of June after a little less than 4 weeks of training. This was a "Depot" division. Their purpose was to collect and house infantry replacement drafts and specialist units like quartermaster groups, signals units, and "Sanitation Trains" of field hospital and ambulance units. The depot units would then funnel the various units to the front line divisions as needed and serve as established camps for replacement drafts as they came ashore.

Assigned to the 303rd Field Hospital of the 301st Sanitation Train, he sailed for France with the division on the SS Aquintiana on July 4th, 1918. They made Liverpool, UK on July 12th, took on provisions and coal, and then landed again at Cherbourg, France on July 16th. The division then encamped St. Amand-Mont-Rond, Chere on July 21st. During it's time there the depot would forward almost 20,000 men through to front line units.

Raymond's unit, the 303rd Field Hospital, was assigned to one of the many camp hospitals that were scattered all over the American rear areas. His was Camp 57 near St. Amand Mont Rond. It was located in portion of the French hospital of that city and occupied two 10-bed wards and four 2-bed rooms. Through the courtesy of the sisters in charge of the hospital the operating room was available for emergency use. On September 1, 1918, the hospital was moved to a building which formerly had been a private school, accommodating about 150 patients. Twelve beds for acute surgical cases were reserved at the French hospital and all operations were performed at there. The number of patients averaged from 120 to 160 at any given time owing to what the British termed "Daily wastage" along the front. It was here they started seeing the wreckage of men coming back from the front.

One patient that came through was PVT Charles Morrow, 304th Field Signal battalion, 79th Div. He was listed as "Gassed and shell shocked." The American army at that time was being mixed in with French units to become acclimated to front line conditions as well as taking up sectors of their own. Snipers, machine guns, trench raids, gas attacks, and artillery barrages were a staple and created a steady stream of injured.

In September, however, bigger things were brewing, namely the major American Meuse–Argonne offensive. 303rd Field Hospital was bumped up to 3rd Corps to be part of the massive hospital system that was being built in the Toul Sector of the Thiaucourt Zone, to support the impending Armageddon. This was a massive network of field and base hospitals extending all the way down to the front. It ultimately hosted the better part of 9,000 beds spread across two base hospitals, two evacuation hospitals, a Red Cross hospital, a Provisional Gas Hospital, a Contagious Disease Hospital, and Neurological Unit No. 2. That was just the corps level facilities. It doesn't count the divisional field hospitals immediately behind the lines. Showing up on the roles of 3rd Corps on September 17th, 303rd Field Hospital with its small staff of 361 personnel, Raymond Brooks from Oxford Maine among them, was swallowed up in a sea of soldiery.

No record I could find details exactly where they went or specifically to who they were assigned. What is certain, however, is that when this battle opened, they got busy. By this stage of the war the Triage system was fairly well perfected. Injured or sick troops would go from point of injury to a forward casualty clearing, or "Dressing" station. They would be initially tended to and then bumped to "Triage" Field Hospitals that sorted by type (gas, wounds, urgent surgical, sickness, etc). From there they were pushed to another FH designated to receive that type of patient. Each infantry division had four FHs organic to their organization for this. Doubtless they were reinforced by the FHs from the depot divisions that were pushed forward in preparation for the coming offensive.

The initial Battle of St. Mihiel was launched on September 11th, 1918. It was a bloody week, but it succeeded at a cost of 8,600 American casualties. Skirmishing, gassing, shelling, and raiding continued, drawing blood every day and night. That set the stage for the Meuse-Argonne Offensive, which commenced on the 28th and raged until the Armistice of November 11, 1918, a total of 47 days. At the time the Meuse–Argonne offensive was the largest in United States military history, involving 1.2 million American soldiers. It is the second deadliest battle in American history, resulting in over 350,000 casualties including 28,000 German lives, 26,277 American lives and an unknown number of French lives. This is where trenches, gas, barbed wire, The Lost Battalion, and shell shock entered the American lexicon.

Somewhere in the middle of this Raymond Brooks got mixed up in it forward enough to get gassed and shell shocked. It's not too difficult to imagine how. The forward hospitals were in full swing as were the dressing station medics and the ambulance companies. Road networks were limited, well mapped and well zero'd by German artillery, as were the trench systems. The dressing stations were getting nailed. The ambulance companies on the roads were getting nailed. The personnel at the division field hospitals were burning out, crushed by the case load and influenza. Send up the new guys from the Depot Divisions, just like they did with the infantry replacements. I have this fragmentary memory from childhood that they got gassed at night. As the division FHs were generally a few miles back, this most likely happened in or around a casualty clearing station on the line. Easy enough for an enlisted guy from a depot fresh FH to get pulled up to replace an ambulance driver or a dressing station medic. Whatever happened, it did enough of a number on him that he spent the rest of his life in the care of his sister, Aunt Anna, and died at age 49.

Lance Corporal Paul Lester Brooks

AEF. U.S. Army Medical Corps

Born in November of 1896, Paul graduated Norway High School class of 1916. He was apparently the HS band marshal. That same year he entered Colby College, eventually graduating Class of 1921. He entered service on July 25th, 1917 along with Hubert.

I believe he initially went through the camp in western Mass. and then to Ft. Benjamin Harrison, Indiana. He then bumped down to the Medical Orderly Training Camp, Camp Greenleaf, Ft. Oglethorpe, GA (located on the Chickamauga-Chattanooga battlefield park). Strangely he is rostered as having come from the Maine National Guard Coastal Artillery detachment. God only knows how much time he spent on trains going back and forth. Stellar Army efficiency in the rush to mobilize, no doubt.

His service card shows “AEF Sept 29, 1918 – July 5th, 1919.” I believe this indicates service in France.

After the war Paul went on to finish Colby in 1921 and then medical school. He is listed as an MD, 1937 Maine Board of Registration of Medicine.

Pvt. Robert Lincoln Brooks

150th Aero Squadron, Rich Field, TX.

The youngest brother, Robert, enlisted on October 17th, 1917. He was 18yrs old. He served with the 150th Aero squadron (later designated Squadron B) at Rich Field, near Waco, TX, being discharged on January 15th, 1919.

This was not a bad billet for a young man at the time. Aviation was in its infancy and the Army Flying Corps was ramping up. “Rich Field was born from an explosion in aeronautics. After a poor performance of US planes in Mexico, President Woodrow Wilson realized that American aircraft were disturbingly inferior to their European counterparts. American planes were slower, had no mounted weaponry, and lacked performance characteristics. Therefore, when the United States entered World War I in April 1917, Wilson approved $640 million to expand the air division of the army (the air force as a separate military unit did not yet exist).” (Anabel Burke, wacohistory.org)

He arrived shortly after the base began operations, with the first shipment of 25 aircraft arriving on November 14. They were uncrated and assembled. Twenty-five flight cadets reported for training on Thanksgiving Day 1917, and flight instruction began on December 1. Eventually a total of 243 Standard J-1 trainers were assigned to Rich Field. In June 1918, the J-1s were replaced by the Curtiss JN-4 “Jenny” which was standardized by the War Department as the training plane for the Air Service. The JN4 would become legendary in American civil aviation serving a multitude of roles and becoming the primary "Barn Storming" aircraft of the 1920s and 30s.

The field turned into a busy place, and eventually some 400 pilots received their wings at Rich Field. As the flight cadets graduated from the six-week course, they were sent to advance schools in the United States, England, or France for training in either pursuit, observation or bomber aircraft. The base newspaper, "The Rich Field Flyer" contains numerous references to their overseas exploits. (Baylor University digital collections)

I'm not sure what he did there, but being around early aviation at that time must have been exciting. Training wings were putting fifty or more planes aloft at a time and I'm sure he was able to grab a ride or two. Crashes were not uncommon and the response crew on the ground were mounted on motorcycles. There was a vaudeville orchestra and the field boasted a football team that played out locally. Weekend passes into nearby Waco were a given, and with 35,000 troops mobilizing at nearby Camp MacArthur, the bar scene must have been crazy. During the flu pandemic in 1918, however, the base quarantined. Suddenly bored, the men started a moustache competition.

All and all it was a pretty rocking place for and young man in the heady days of WW1 and a hell of a lot nicer than the charnel house of the hospitals in France.

After the war the census of 1920 shows he returned to live with his parents and was working as a steamfitter in a factory.

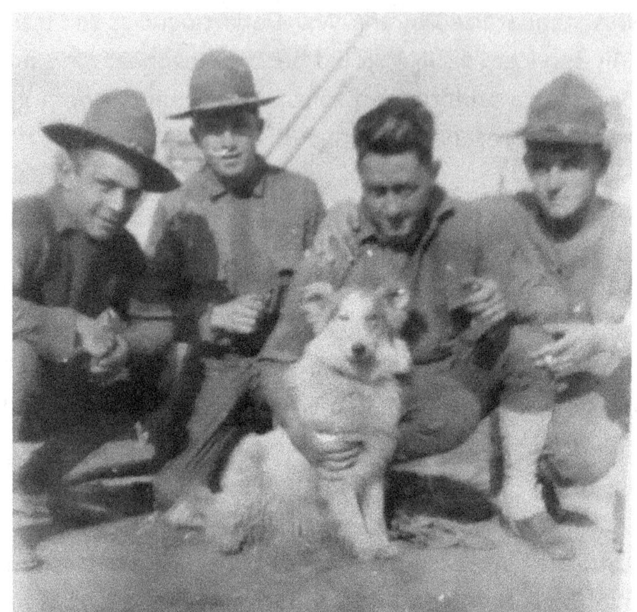

The Brooks boys go to war. Like thousands of other men from New England they mustered in and received their first rudimentary training at Camp Devens, Massachusetts.

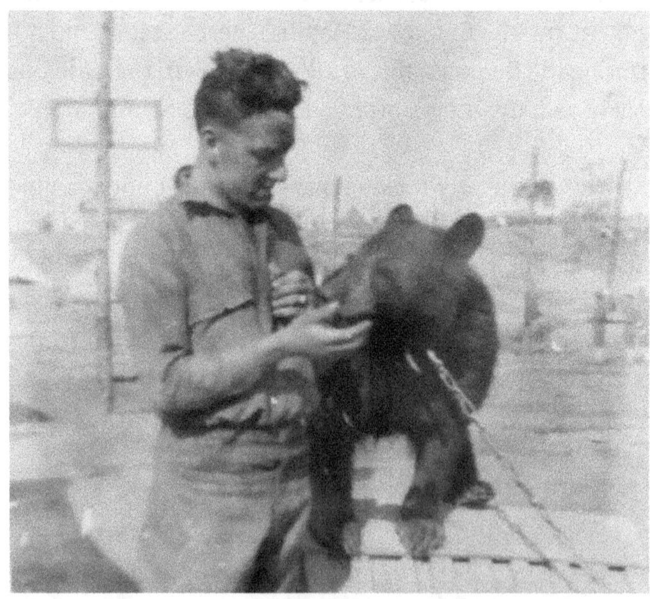

Grandpa Hubert Brooks with a pet bear Camp Zachary Taylor.

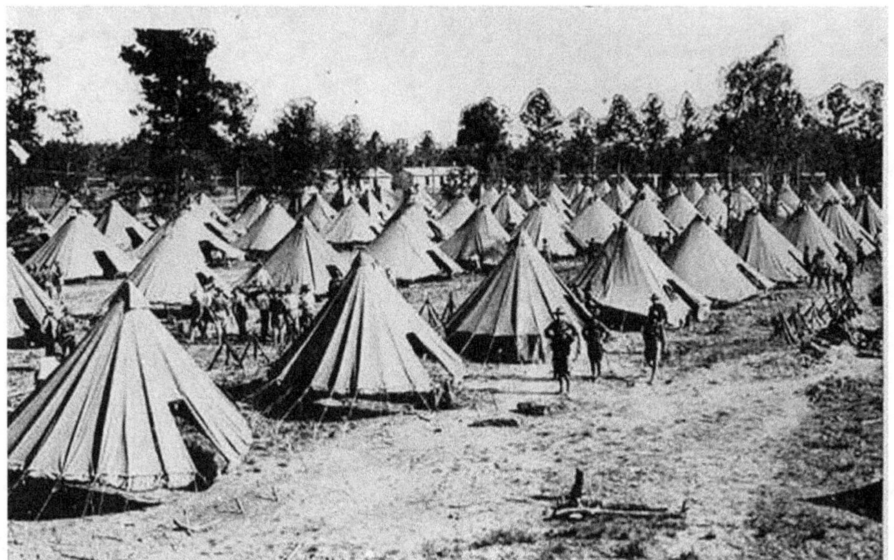

Camp Oglethorpe, GA. Hastily expanded as the US mobilized, on posts like Oglethorpe the pioneer battalions erected massive tent cities for incoming troops. Despite improved sanitation standards, the Influenza of 1918 would keep the medical detachments extremely busy.

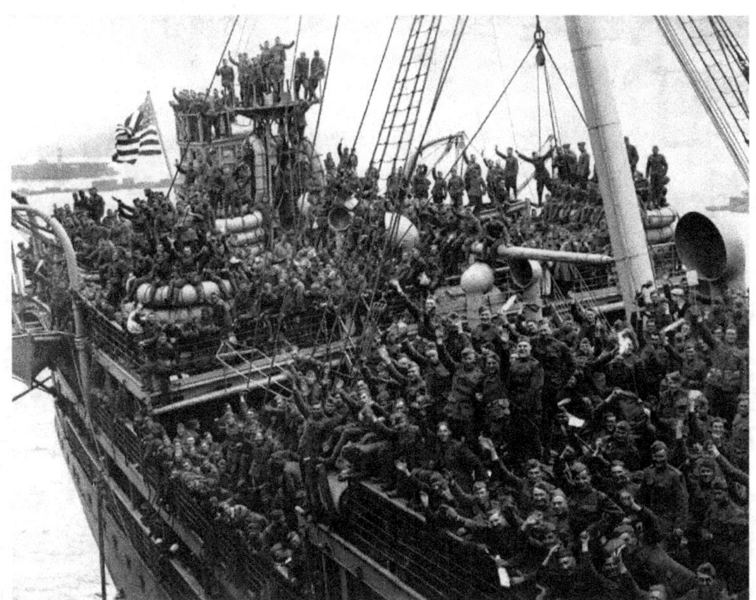

American troops embarking for France. Packed ships like these posed additional challenges for the Medical Department.

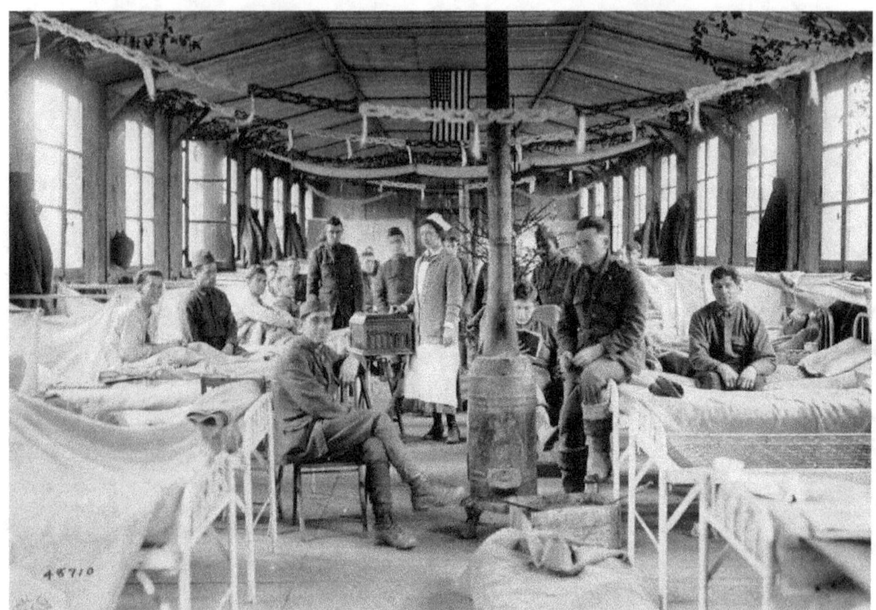

U.S. base hospital somewhere in France, 1918. An extensive network of facilities lowered military death rates to levels never before seen, even with influenza. From 18.9% of combatants in the Civil War down to 2.5% of U.S. combatants in France.

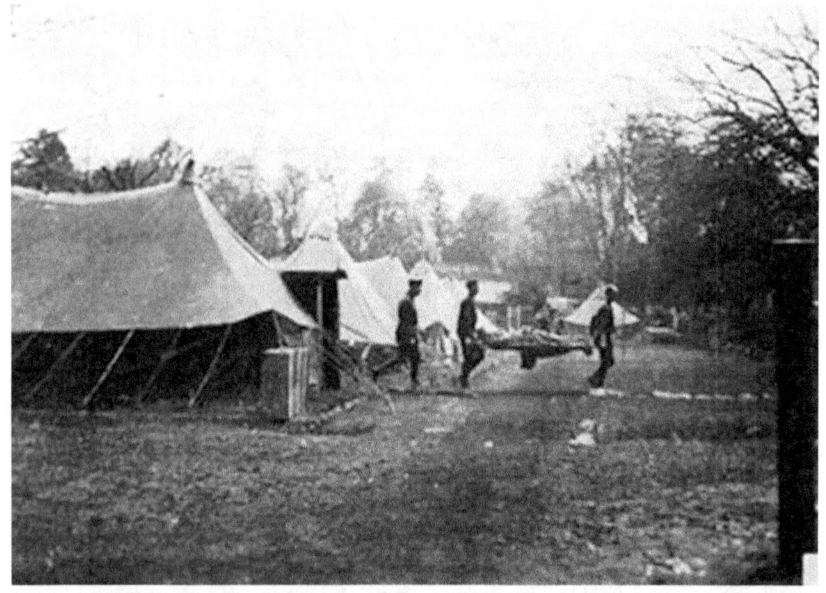

Field hospital in France. Rapid triage and emergency surgery at these hospitals just behind the front meant survival for most who made it there.

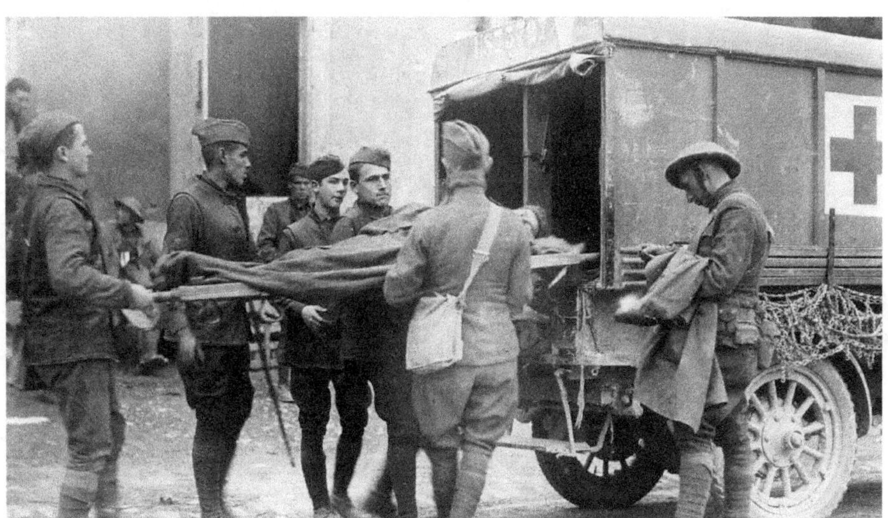

A U.S. Ambulance delivers a patient to a forward field hospital somewhere in France, 1918. Motorization of this branch revolutionized battlefield evacuation and brought death rates to historic lows.

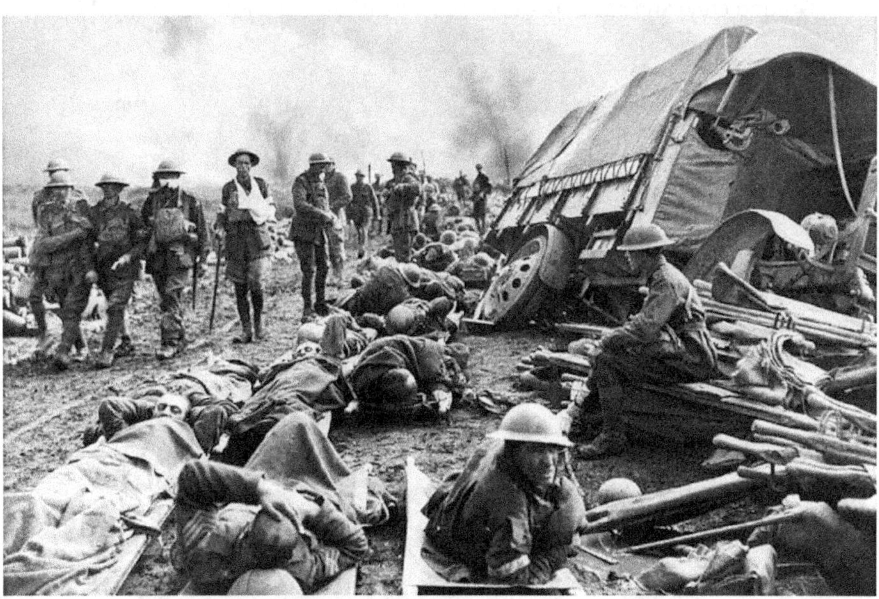

Casualty clearing point on the front. The extended range of modern artillery made these a dicey place to be.

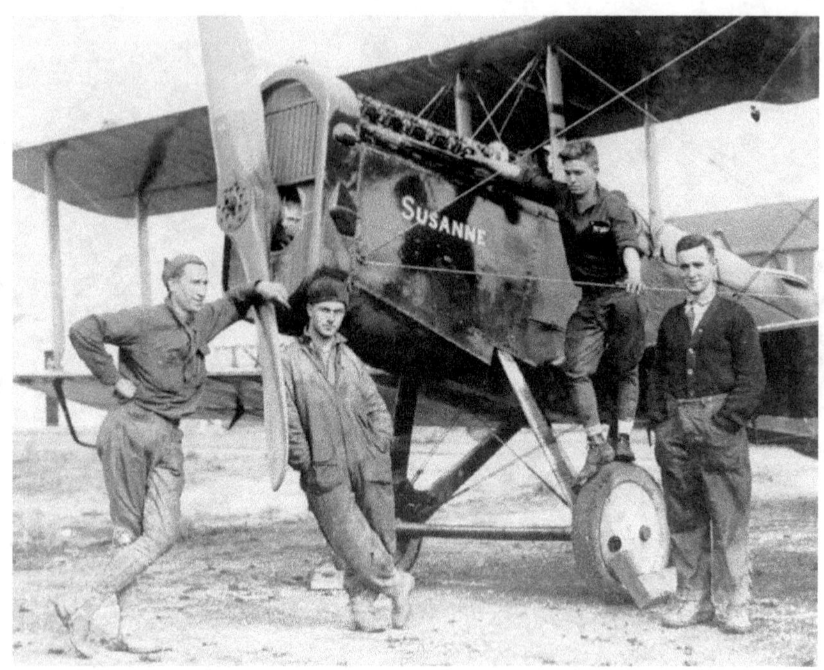

Ground crew and cadet pilots pose with a Curtis JN4. Rich Field, TX. 1918.

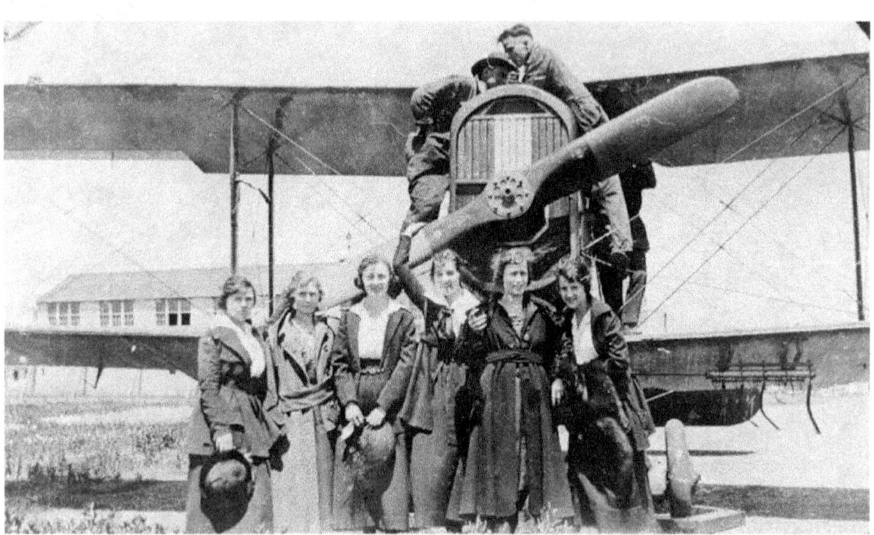

Visitors to Rich Field. Waco, TX became a bustling city as the mobilization camp and flight school brought in thousands of people to the sleepy, dusty town. Not a bad billet for Robert, the youngest of the Brooks clan.

Other Notables

Sometimes you get to have a number of "fathers." I was fortunate in this regard and their various influences left their mark as well.

Keep 'em Coming: Homefront Shipyards WW2

Josephine Bartlett (Nana)

"Nana" came into our line when she married Grandpa Skipper on April 22nd, 1948. (Skipper's first wife and dad's mother, Madge, having passed away while Dad was on Okinawa in 1945.)

She worked in the South Portland Shipyard during WW2. She worked in steam fitting division building Liberty Ships as a pipefitter. Her primary duty was to sew canvas coverings over the insulation around the steam pipes. She used large, curved needles which I still have.

3,700 women worked in the yard during the war, earning on average $1.20 an hour, working six days a week. What became the New England Shipbuilding Corporation produced 266 ships during the war at the East and West Yard.

Housing was tight during that time because so many people showed up so quickly to build ships for the war. I recall she roomed with four or five other girls. There were the "Rosie the riveters" and "Wendy the welders" that helped win the logistics campaign of a global war.

With 13 total "ways" where the ships were assembled, the yards in Portland were one of the larger concerns in the nation. Overall something like 30,000 workers came into the ship building yards during this time. It was a big, dangerous, beehive of activity with Liberty Ships in particular being built and launched at a rapid pace due to their modular design (a major piece of American WW2 innovation). The SS Jerimiah O'Brien, which is still afloat in San Francisco as a museum ship, was built here.

Pvt. Charles Milliken Brooks

U.S. Army Air Corps. 1943-44

Uncle Charlie was momma Betty's brother. He enlisted in the US Army Air Corps on 26 Feb. 1943, at Miami Beach, FL. If I recall correctly he was training to be a navigator or a gunner on B-25 Mitchells. There's nto a lot in his service records that I could find.

I believe ultimately he was injured in an air crash during training in NC. and was medically discharged. He passed away before I was born, but the first camera I ever used was his old Kodak, fully manual 35mm with split image range finder. I still have it.

Mildred "Millie" Taylor

Keep 'em Flying: Homefront WW2

Millie became my mother's stable manager and stayed with her until she passed away in the mid-90s. She came from a small farm in Ohio and one story she told was her father's battle with his mules. He was plowing and they decided that they had had enough and sat down.

Good luck moving them, so he walked back to the farm house, leaving them there. After a while he saw them standing up so he walked back out. As he approached, they sat down. This went on until sunset. He finished the field the next day.

She recalled that even during the Depression she didn't really know they were poor as they had daily work to do and had everything they really needed from the farm.

When WW2 broke out she went to the big city and began working in a factory that was making drop tanks for P-47s.

Dennis Jordan

2nd Infantry, Korea, late 1950s.

The Jordan's, Dennis and Dinah, were our immediate neighbor and I grew up spending a lot of time there. It is told that Dinah once found myself and her daughter, Mandy, in a big mud puddle in their driveway. We told her we were learning to swim. As for Dennis, he was a larger than life figure. He was a dead ringer for the guy who played Daniel Boone on TV at the time and in many ways he really was a Daniel Boone.

He was a farrier and a trapper and they had a huge old barn where he had his trapper shed. The whole place was filled with the most fascinating things. I have no doubt that this influence steered me towards an early interest in mountain men and "Buckskinning." I have said on many an occasion that while my dad gave me medicine, running a farm, and the patrolling skills of a cavalry officer, Dennis made me a woodsman. The stealthy ways of the Iroquois, the steady, single shot precision required of a black powder long rifle, the sensibility of studying the habits of animals in their natural environment, and how to be a tracker. He also turned me on to gathering sustenance from the bounty of the Maine woods. Between him and Tom Brown's Field Guides, I became very adept at the latter two, and between him and Dad, an accomplished marksman.

All these things would contribute to my survival in one way or another across the various places I got myself into in later years. He also taught me how to swear, he and another old blacksmith on the track named Peanut Millet. It is a habit I unfortunately carry to this day, but oh well. My poor step mother Betty was mortified, but what were you going to do.

I remember he took Dennis McCann and I ice fishing one year on some river somewhere. We caught a pile of smelts. He told us we couldn't be real ice fishermen until we had bitten the head off a smelt, so we did. He taught us how to snowshoe a trapline, throw a hatchet, and work metal and leather. At one point he got a black and tan hound and we had a number of adventures smashing through the woods at night chasing raccoons. I can't recall that we ever killed one, but we did tree a few. It was a series of little toughing up exercises the whole time I lived next door to him.

There was also the one and only time I ever shot a deer. Dad had me take it down to Dennis and we processed it in his basement. The juxtaposition to all this, at the same time, was that he always had some kind of baby animal around, like squirrels, birds, and chipmunks, that he had rescued and would hand raise in the kitchen. There was a whole pack of them that would take up residence around the house and live there.

I remember another time Steve Brown and I were playing around down in the big gravel pit off Bald Hill Road and we found a fox caught in a trap, out of season. We tried to approach it, but it was understandably snarling and dangerous. So we ran, and I mean ran, the better part of two miles to Dennis's place and alerted him. He piled us into his green truck and we went back. He just walked over and calmly picked the thing up by the chain, pressed the spring and freed it. He told me later that it had ultimately lost its foot but grew a pad over the stump, and he would see his peg leg tracks for a number of years thereafter.

He would actively stoke any kind of interest in these sorts of Boys Adventure Activity things. There was one phase where I was all into studying early medieval cannons so I went to our barn and found a piece of pipe. I knocked out a wooden mount for it and secured it with bent over nails. Gathering up my powder horn and a bucket of crab apples, I snuck down into their barn and took up position on the second floor. From there I loaded it up with crab apples and touched it off with a lit cigarette, shooting them at the house. It's a miracle I didn't burn the place down. After a pretty good barrage but no response from inside I slid down there and obtusely asked if they had heard anything hitting the house. Dinah immediately asked, "What have you been doing?" I, of course, fessed up straight away. "Well go get the thing, I want to see it," Dennis says. Impressed with the initiative he told me to leave it with him and come back tomorrow. The next day I returned and he had welded a plug onto the back and drilled a proper touch hole. It became a regular feature at our school pep rallies and I still have it. Ah, growing up in the days before bike helmets and Homeland Security.

He talked a bit about his service in Korea as well. He was there in the late fifties, after the major fighting was over and the Army had upgraded to the M-14. Despite the truce the DMZ in Korea was still a very dangerous place. North Korea sent wave after wave of infiltrators south and there were constant skirmishes across the line. “They’d come across at night in tennis shoes and you couldn’t hear the bastards,” he said. “They’d creep up to our bunkers and try to get a grenade in there. Couple guys I knew got busted up pretty bad. None of us got a lot of sleep up there.”

Years later I was in Arizona running with the Border Patrol. We were out in the middle of nowhere, at night, in the desert west of Tucson tracking a group of about a dozen. There’s lots of traffic in that area and there are swarms of tracks everywhere. The big problem is differentiating what’s from an hour ago and what’s from six hours ago. I had a suspicion we were drifting off the fresh set of tracks so I ducked back a ways and gently blew into each of the tracks. In the one set a tiny cloud of super fine dust rose up, but not in the others. Those were the fresh ones. I showed the BP agent I was with and we set off following the correct set.

The next morning they asked me where I learned to cut sign so good. The answer was simple, “I Grew up in New Gloucester, Maine next door to an old blacksmith trapper named Dennis Jordan.”

Joe McClung

U.S. Naval Aviator 1945-6

Joe came into my world as a stepfather from about age 8 through 14. He was a big guy, handsome, had a commanding presence but a gentle demeanor. He was an architect and he and my mom built this big place down in Florida where I would go visit in the summers. We did a lot of dirt bike riding back then. I had this tiny Honda MR50, my mom had a blue Penton, and he had this big old Ossa. It had a shamrock logo on it and it was the coolest thing.

I was on the place one day and they were out riding. I looked up and here they came back, but with Joe towing mom on the Penton. She had mistaken a full blown cow pond for a big puddle and thinking she was going to "skim right across it" had sunk the thing in seven or eight feet of water. Joe, of course, went swimming and got the thing hooked to a tow rope and got it out. They were both soaked and covered in cow plop flakes, but this was legit hero stuff in my eyes. He took charge and solved the problem.

He also had one of the first legit Corvette C3 Stingrays, a big orange thing that we would go cruising in with the T-top removed. I remember well the engine in that thing, a big, rumbling V8. This was a big departure from the rigid New England practicality of station wagons and sedans we had in Maine. That thing was a fighter jet.

Of course it was, Joe had been a Naval Aviator in the closing days of WW2. Originally from Kansas, he had grown up around the oil fields as his dad was a wildcat driller and oilman. Little wonder the thought of big oceans, open skies, and the challenge of air to air combat appealed to him. He had trained at Pensacola and Jacksonville, qualifying as a carrier pilot in Grumman F6F Hellcats. In short order he was on his way to the Pacific.

To his surprise, however, he wasn't assigned to a carrier group but instead to a wing based at Henderson Field on Guadalcanal. There they were engaged in long range patrols, and for a short time mopping up the remnants of Japanese shipping and coastal forces around the Solomon Islands. The war rapidly drew to a close from there. On Guadalcanal, however, there was still no small amount of danger lurking. He related to me stories of Japanese stragglers and hold outs who would periodically attack the base. He said that they had actually lost a few men who had strayed away from the airfield alone, looking for souvenirs. It was very quickly forbidden for anyone to go outside the wire in groups of less than five and heavily armed. Another threat were the swarms of stray dogs that had been loosed on the island. They had quickly gone feral and roamed in packs, occasionally attacking the unwary down by the beaches. Word went out to cull the packs and in their down time they would roll out in jeeps on dog hunting expeditions. Flare guns were a particularly favored weapon as was the Thompson submachine gun.

Joe imparted a lot of small habits that I carry with me to this day. Things like making your bed in the morning and washing the excess tooth paste out of the sink when you're finished brushing your teeth. These may sound a bit OCD, but they really are the foundation of the habit of paying attention to details. Whether coming in to land on a rocking postage stamp in the middle of an ocean or designing a modern building, attention to details becomes pretty damn important. I'm sure it was the same in the dangerous world of oil wells he grew up in.

When I got to Ft. Leonard Wood years later our drill instructors hammered this in. "Attention to detail, troop, attention to detail!" I had to smile, as it made me think of Joe. For me it became especially true in the theatre of ground war. You have got to pay attention to the little details that are unfolding around you at all times. From a neighborhood in Iraq where the people are not out on the street like they were yesterday, to the three tiny prongs of a PROM-1 landmine barely visible in the grass, attention to details is what gets you home.

Every morning when I wash the excess toothpaste out of the sink, or I wipe down the stove top after I'm done cooking, I think of Joe.

Col. Carl F. Bernard

USMC WW2 to Senior Province Advisor, Vietnam

Carl Bernard was the most important mentor I could have ever come by going into my adult years. He was a consummate warrior, academic, and quiet statesman. As I say, my Dad made sure I was a competent horseman and medic, but Bernard finished me as an intellectual. He was the deepest, most intellectually dialed in person I ever had the privilege of working with, and did so for the better part of fifteen years as his adjutant / aide de camp whenever I was home.

I came into Bernard's world by a complete fluke. I was over in Croatia, running with 105 and 108 Brigades of the HV. We had been having the summer of discontent down in a hotly contested pocket in Northern Bosnia that summer. I knew some people around Zagreb, including the resident Newsweek stringer, Joel. I was hanging out over at his place one day and he offhandedly mentioned that he was going to be going down to Sarajevo for a week, shepherding some associate editor from the magazine. I asked offhand who it was, maybe I know their byline.

"Some guy named David Hackworth," he replied, clearly not knowing who this was. "What!! David Hackworth is coming here?!" I shouted back excitedly. Joel was a bit taken aback, as admittedly I was a rebel outlier to him. (he was one of those journos who wore shorts and dock siders while running around under the siege of Sarajevo. Nice guy, but not cut from the soldier cloth) I hastily explained who epic warrior rebel Col. David Hackworth was. Joel continued to look at me skeptically.

You see I knew Dave Hackworth in a big way. I got my hands on a first edition of his groundbreaking work "About Face" wherein he broke down the world of soldiering between the rouge warriors and the careerist bureaucrats, and his adventures sticking it to them over the years. At the time he had the most decorations of any living veteran alive, all of them legit combat awards. I had carried my copy of "About Face" first to basic training / AIT at Ft. Leonard Wood and then to Croatia and Bosnia. It was literally dog eared and riding around in my ruck sack. I begged Joel to set up an introduction. Predictably, he obfuscated. I knew Joel wasn't going to hook me up, I was unfit to be around his polite society of "professional" journalists. Never mind we were all in our early 20s and most of these journalists didn't know shit from shineola when it came to war. No matter. Out-flanking him was going to be easy enough.

I knew that he had to bring Hackworth to the Croatian Press Office in the Intercontinental hotel to get his media credentials. So on the day Hack arrives I stake the place out, all day. I waited for hours and towards 5pm I had pretty much given up. As I started out the side door I thought that maybe I could give it one more chance and walk out the front of the hotel. I turned around, started for the lobby and there was Joel and the Col. David Hackworth walking towards me. "Hi Joel," I smiled. Good sport that he was, he just chuckled and grinned. Then I turned and said;

"Are you Col. Hackworth?"
"Why yes, I am. Dave Hackworth. Who are you?"
I come to attention, salute and say, "Corporal Bartlett, B Company of the 229th Engineers, it's an honor to meet you, Sir!"
"The 229th, is that part of the 29th Infantry Division?"
"Why yes sir it is, The Blue and the Gray."
He lights up. "Why my old commander Glover Johns was in the 29th Infantry in Normandy."
"Yes sir he was, Clay Pigeons of St. Lo, read it when I was 15."
"That's most excellent. What are you doing int his place?" he asks.
"Well, sir. They wanted to send me to OCS, but all this broke out and I felt if I was going to be a decent officer I had better get some combat under my belt. So I'm down here and have gotten mixed in with these Croatian Army units down in Bosanski Brod."

Now Hackworth was not one to miss out on a good source so he asks me what I was doing that evening. Dinner was quickly arranged and later that evening I was at the Esplanade telling him all about my adventures with the Hrvatski Vojska and in the Posavina corridor battlefield. This intrigues him to no end. He has to go down to Sarajevo for a week with Joel, but in the meantime assigns me to take the Newsweek car and go down to Brod and make arrangements for him to visit. This turns into Jim's grand adventure with David Hackworth in Bosnia where I took him down to the front. We got the snot shelled out of us, he uncovers this whole thing about smuggled South African Milan anti-tank missiles, and I generally have the time of my life with this major hero of mine. Shortly thereafter, Hack returned to the US but was caught up in the whole Admiral Boorda clusterfuk and exited journalism for good. Thusly I have the distinct honor of being the last person ever to soldier with David Hackworth on an active battlefield.

Our relationship continued, however, and when I returned home I met up with him again in Richmond, being his driver and horse holder for some event he was attending. He said he had an old friend up in Alexandria who could use a guy like me and that is how I came to be Col. Carl Bernard's adjutant. The two of them went way back to Vietnam. Hackworth was the rebel and Bernard, equally combat tested, was the quieter, more diplomatic one. It was one of those chance meetings that changes the trajectory of one's personal development, even though you might not know it at the time.

Here is a brief synopsis of his life. It is initial draft of his obituary that I wrote for the Washington Post in March of 2008.

"Carl was born on May 31st, 1926 in Borger, TX and grew up in the oil fields and work towns of the west during the Great Depression. From 1944 to 1946 he served in the Pacific and China as an enlisted US Marine before enlisting the US Army in 1947. He went on to retire as a full Colonel and was considered one of the most deeply intellectual men the army produced during the Cold War and Vietnam eras.

In 1948 Cpl Bernard was made an honorary member of the 555th "Triple Nickel," an all African American parachute regiment. After being assigned to discover why the men of that unit did poorly on standardized army tests, he discovered it was a simple case of no one having ever taught them to take such tests. Bernard launched a program for test-

taking skills and soon the unit was achieving some of the highest aggregate test scores in the army. Carl was a regular feature at their reunions over the years.

Following his commission as an infantry officer in 1949 Lt. Bernard was stationed in Japan as a platoon leader with L Co. 21st Infantry. On July 1st 1950 Bernard had the misfortune of being sent to the Kokura Airfield to help COL. Charles B. Smith's task force load for their trip to Korea several days after the North Korean invasion of the south. Told by Smith to "Stay on the plane, I've got work for you," he was with "Task Force Smith" at Osan five days later when it was overrun by the North Koreans. In the aftermath Lt. Bernard led a group of survivors from behind enemy lines and back to American positions a week later.

He was reunited with L Co., and several days later was overrun again at Chochiwan, where Lt. Bernard was awarded the Distinguished Service Cross for his actions during a close combat melee with North Korean tanks. His unit had been deployed to Korea with weapons tagged "Combat Unserviceable," and despite heroic efforts all around, the N. Koreans drove them into Pusan. Later in life Bernard would become a tireless advocate for Army readiness based on this experience.

Following Korea, Bernard served in numerous posts including a company command in Germany, Ranger School at Ft Benning, GA, and attended the Command and General Staff College at Ft. Leavenworth, KS. Things really started getting interesting, however, when he was assigned to help develop the curriculum at the newly formed John F. Kennedy Special Warfare School at Fort Bragg, NC. Class development proved to be brief and Bernard shortly found himself with notable CIA figure Bill Colby amongst the H'Mong hill tribes of Laos in 1960 as part of the White Star Mobile Training Teams. Here he developed an affinity for the H'Mong people and until the end of his life was a tireless advocate for them and unceasing critic of the US Government's abandonment of them to the Pathet Lao Communists after the fall of Saigon.

After his time in Laos, Bernard returned to the Special Warfare School at Ft. Bragg, focusing on revolutionary movements and insurgency warfare. He was sent to attend the French Ecole D'Etat Major, in Paris, and later served on NATO staff positions in Germany. In 1967, John Paul Vann recruited Bernard to come to Vietnam as the Province Senior Advisor in Hau Nghia (home of the infamous Tunnels of Cu Chi) and later Vinh Binh province.

An early expert on counterinsurgency warfare, Bernard clashed constantly with "maneuver" generals convinced that artillery and tanks were the answer to their guerilla war problems. Despite this, Bernard made great strides in rural development and pacification during his 2 years in Vietnam, and was repeatedly decorated for his efforts. Vietnam proved to be less of a challenge then his last assignment, however, which was restoring Army ROTC to the campus at UC Berkeley.

When COL Bernard arrived at Berkeley in the fall of 1972, he strode, in full uniform, straight into the tumultuous epicenter of the anti-Vietnam War movement. Under Federal pressure to restore the ROTC program, the school presented a less than welcoming face to the decorated Vietnam war Colonel. He was consigned to the basement of an athletic building to run the program, where he gently began revamping it. Declaring a slew of courses unfit to receive Berkeley academic credit, he turned heads by ridding the ROTC curriculum of what he considered to be Army "Basket Weaving" classes. This won him early allies, and over time he quietly wove in topics ranging from the Hegelian Dialectic to social justice in armed conflict.

As his academic career progressed, his tableau of speaking topics, such as Che Guevarra on Revolutionary War, became some of the most popular lectures on campus. By the time Bernard retired, he had gone from the basement to lecturing before standing room only auditoriums that included some of the most notable campus radicals of the day. He repeatedly said over the years that winning the hearts and minds of UC Berkeley was his proudest achievement.

Following his retirement from the Army in 1978, he settled in the Washington, DC area and ran a consulting firm specializing in Army readiness and US-French military relations. He continued to be a tireless advocate for H'mong refugees, the environment, and social alternatives to armed conflict. Spending more time online and in his e-mail than most teenagers, his words and wisdom have been circulated widely and at the highest levels.

Bernard received a B.A. in Asian Studies from Kansas State University, an M.A. from Boston University, and completed doctoral coursework at UC Berkeley."

I wasn't kidding when I said he finished me as an intellectual. I mean, where the hell to start? I came into his world while I was in my early 20s, coming out of my first international conflict. He left us when I was in my early forties. When I was home I was working in his office, handling correspondence, editing and filing the innumerable papers he wrote, and acted as coordinator and host for any number of people that were constantly coming and going from the place in Mt. Vernon. That was a scene. Everyone from SEAL Team 6 Dick Marcinco to Montgomery McFate, founder of the Human Terrain Mapping program, came through there. You can imagine what it must have been like to sit on the back deck and listen to him and Marcinco riff on special operations, terrorism, and counter insurgency topics. My brain was melting most days.

He would entreat with almost anyone. People were heard, they were encouraged, mentored, and connected. This went on for decades and he quietly moved a lot of things along in DC circles. It didn't become apparent until we buried him at Arlington just how diverse this set of lives he touched was. There was the better part of 400 people there. They had to use tour buses to bring everyone down to the staging area from where we followed the caisson, the riderless horse, the full band, and a full rifle company from the Old Guard. There was everyone there from the old lefty, hippy profs he knew from Berkley to an honor guard from 5th Group US Special Forces who came up from Ft. Campbell, led by a Lieutenant Colonel. I hadn't known the half of it the whole time.

Thesis & Antithesis

One of the most important thing he ever laid on me, however, was "Hegel's Dialectics." As he described it, it involved the concept of thesis, anti-thesis, and synthesis. Initially, for every viewpoint there will be an equally opposite one, from every possible angle. In order to see the full spectrum and all the details of an issue you have to engage in that process of thinking. From there you can begin to work through the more simplistic arguments and refine them, one at a time, down into the complexities of it. That's where you will find the solutions, the path forward, or a decision to abandon that track. To engage in this process embodies the essence of being able to "see the world through someone elses eyes." It was a good fit for me because working with animals involves the same process, as they can't speak and tell you what's up. You have to sus it out through their signals and being able to see through their eyes. Bernard was a master of this, and combined with his considerable charm and grace, enabled him to get people to see things as he did and get them to do what he wanted to do. It wasn't manipulation. You wanted to do whatever he asked because you knew he understood where you were coming from and he shared similar outlooks.

Paper Stays

He was always sending faxes. Even when we came fully into the world of email, he sent faxes when it counted. There were over a dozen law office sized filing cabinets in the basement of Mt. Vernon, every one of them full of correspondence, papers, and their corresponding fax cover sheets. I asked once why he would do that when he could just send things as an attachment. "Paper stays," he said. I looked at him puzzled and he expounded. He said, "An email can be easily dismissed, deleted or overlooked. Paper, however, sits on a desk until it is dealt with. It stays."

Boy, did he have DCs racket pegged. Years later, just before he died, he moved over to the Ft. Belvoir retirement community. I drew the task of going through each cabinet, saving the most important things. I mean, I knew there was interesting stuff in there, but when I started digging in I started finding solid gold, stuff that needed to be in the Army archives.

Here's one example; He's in Vietnam, working for John Paul Vann, the pacification guru the Army failed to listen to. They're trying to pacify Viet Cong hot spot Haugh Nhia Province. He and Vann are going back and forth via telex about all the various incidents that were happening between troops from the 1st Infantry and the locals. Little things that weren't helping the cause, like parking your M113 APC next to a villagers house, drinking, and then throwing a grenade at their dog because it barked at you.

Bernard figures that all this stuff might be interesting later so he tears them off the machine, initials and scratches off "Classified" in the header, stuffs it all into envelopes, and mails it back to a friend in DC for safe keeping. Here it is fifty years later in his file cabinets. Next cabinet over is lengthy correspondence between he and Colin Powell, all of it on paper and faxed. The whole basement was like this. I, having a keen eye for historical material, filled nine bankers' document boxes with the most precious stuff. He still had a hand typed copy of the original officer's curriculum he wrote for the JFK Special Warfare School in like 1958.

One big mystery was solved, however, when I found the file he kept on me. Whenever I was overseas in some place he would always make sure I wrote to keep him informed and would ask me to look into some things here and there. I didn't think much of it, if kindly old Carl wanted me to write something up for him, of course.

So I ask him, "Hey Carl, on all of my emails there's a fax transmission sheet. Where did you send all this?"
"Well, some I sent to friends up in Mclean, and most of the Bosnia stuff to the White House," he replies.

"The White House?"
"Yes, a couple girls who interned for me were working for Leon Panetta, so I sent it to them."
"So the letter I sent when I figured out the Serbs were staying off the tactical radio and broadcasting orders in the open over their TV and radio in Serbian nightclub slang went to Panetta?"
"Yes. Your perceptions were very useful."
"You could have told me you were doing this, I'd have used the F-word a little less!"
"No, it was perfect as it was. You were so raw they knew it was real. They knew you weren't trying to play some beltway angle."

Evidently, because a couple weeks after I sent that, US planes started bombing Serb radio and TV stations. Shortly thereafter our planes over Kosovo actually started hitting what they were aiming at, which they had failed to do for nearly 70 days, the Serbs always skating out from under them at the last minute. This new paradigm imploded the Serbian campaign there, prompting their withdrawal.

Paper stays indeed.

Truth is Perception

I forget what I was going on about one day. Probably the mindset of the Serbs and their idea that it was all a conspiracy against them and they never did anything wrong. I can't remember, but in his gentle or sometimes firm way, Carl brought it to the point...the truth is what people believe it to be. He was way ahead of the "my personal truth" buzz word. Ultimately, however, it's a very old human response and that's why the Hegelian Thesis was so important. Only through careful and measured, step by step dissection of an issue could you move the slider on the perception scale, starting with your own. Then you begin with acknowledging where someone is coming from and then let the Hegelian Dialectic to do its work.

Crystallization of Key Concepts, and Repeat

Once he had distilled the issue down into the heart of the matter, he would construct a set of key points and repeat them. This was especially apparent in the work he did regarding Army readiness. He was able to draw on his own experience in Korea when he had been Shanghai'd onto Smith's bird and dropped squarely into what became the Task Force Smith disaster. In the rush to pack up the end of WW2 in the Pacific, very little had been done to ensure that equipment met combat standards. (Hell, half the time they didn't even correctly label the crates they packed the stuff up in. They'd open up a crate marked "Cold weather hats" and bayonets would fall out.) When they left for the airport, most of the weapons they had drawn from the armory were tagged "Combat Unserviceable," suitable for parade props but little else. In the post-war era of "This won't happen ever again" no one had thought to replace them with rifles that worked. A lot of guys died because of that oversight.

"There are no second chances on a battlefield. You are ready, or you are not. It can't be pencil whipped in a report or an armory book. If you are not, men die." This was a key concept and he repeated over and over. Over the years, because of his wide web of relationships, there was a veritable army of people wandering the Pentagon that carried that message. Despite some shortcomings when we hit Iraq in 2003 (something he didn't support), you could see where this had sunk in on a number of levels. He by no means took any huge amount of credit for this, but having mentored any number of young officers over the years, I have no doubt that his contribution was larger than most. Simple, easy to grasp, easy to repeat. A readiness meme before the concept of memes existed.

Another common refrain he used was from the Stouffer Study that came out after WW2 that examined every aspect of our operations during the war. From the comparative number of rounds in combat fired by different units, to the performance of specific recruit categories, the Stouffer study examined it all. In its assessment of personnel, they noted the Army's bad habit of assigning category 4Fs to the infantry, while sending the smart ones to radar schools and such. They icily concluded, "Assigning a stupid man to the infantry was tantamount to sentencing him to death."

You Won't be Seated at the Table if You're Outside Throwing Rocks.

I was going on and on about something, still young, spooled up about some view or policy the Clinton Administration was up to. Carl gently listened, injected views with his usual, sage wisdom. But, being young, I continued. He finally brought his hand down on the table. "How can you expect to be at the table where the decisions are being made if you're outside throwing stones? If you're not at that table you have no input on the course of events," he said firmly.

Instant epiphany. That's why he was so effective in DC for so many years. He could sit and entreat with anyone, very rarely, if ever, allowing his own views to interfere. Combined with his innate charm and his ability to leverage the Hegelian Dialectic, there was rarely a table he wasn't seated at. It's a lesson many in our present day discourse might apply to themselves.

Atomic Theory of Change

Rarely does the human race make big change quickly. Whenever it has, it usually doesn't end well and is rife with unintended consequences. "Revolutions" are rarely clean or even effective in the long run at addressing the problems they set out to solve. "We're all particles floating through this space. We come into contact with each other and each contact has a small effect on the other, changing their trajectory slightly. It is only over time that you see where the new trajectory takes people. Radical change is not something humans manage very well," he said.

In this sphere he understood that being tempered, thoughtful, deliberate, and inclusive in your views and actions was important at all times. The ultimate effect will rarely be apparent immediately, but would slowly ripple out over time. We don't "Move" events or perceptions, we "Nudge" them.

His sense of this early on was shown when he was assigned to find out why the African-American soldiers of the 55th Airborne were doing poorly on the army tests, a requirement for their full integration into the armed forces. Bernard, in his even, tempered, and fair way first broke bread with them to find out why this was the case. "These men are not stupid, they're some of the finest troops I've ever commanded," he was told by the unit's CO. As he quietly formed a relationship with them he discovered that the root of the issue was that no one had ever instructed them on how to take these kinds of exams. In short order he put together a curriculum and taught it. The men of that unit went fourth and scored some of the highest marks in the history of the tests. No small number of those men went on, over the following decades, and achieved very high rank, making their presence felt across a very broad spectrum. The history of integration in the armed forces has not been without its setbacks, but by and large it was a leader in that realm for the larger society. This in no small measure came from the excellent Troopers the 555th had attracted to the ranks and the Army retained. One little nudge, at the right time, in the right place, with the right people. Classic Bernard.

At no point was this more evident than at his funeral, when the dedicated Berkley lefty stood side by side with the Special Forces officer to pay their respects to this man.

Did I mention that he finished me as a thinker and an intellectual?

James B. Johnson

102nd NJ Cavalry and US Army Air Corps WW2

My maternal grandfather was James Johnson. When WW2 came along he was older and married to my grandmother Frances, so that meant it was going to be a stateside billet for him. As I understand it he was commissioned as a major, and sent to teach radar at a school in Florida. Grandmother was kinda flush, so his uniform was tailored and his rank insignia, etc, was struck at Tiffany's in NY.

They met through the horse circuit. He had been a member of NJ's famous "Essex Troop" which was a Hussar unit that was part of the NJ guard as the 102nd Cavalry. I still have his Hussar hat and uniforms.

Jim was a tall, very good looking guy and very gregarious. This would explain him and my grandmother, who was pretty high up on the food chain herself. He became a sports reporter and was a regular fixture of the horse and the sports world. His circle of friends included pretty much anyone who was notable in those worlds back then.

He had a way of working a room and making everyone feel as if they were special, even if he didn't know their name. "Hey there, good to see you, good to see you," was a standard greeting.

I remember when I was in my early teens and we were visiting he gave me several WW2 items he had acquired, including a very ornate Japanese dagger. I was flabbergasted and tried to refuse. He looked at me sternly and said, "Be gracious and accept."

Be gracious, and accept. I never forgot that. He embodied that sense of social decorum. While I have never mastered it on his level, it has been a useful influence.

Postscript

It was a given that I was, sooner or later, going to find myself in a conflict zone. This was by no means deliberate on my father's part, but it was equally inevitable. It was a set of footsteps I was bound to follow. The footsteps of my fathers. The consciousness of the experiences of my own ancestors and others, seeping in over the years, became a force that would draw me to it. From an early age I studied these experiences, becoming pretty well versed in them.

I remember being asked why I was going to join the Guard and go off to Ft. Leonard Wood. My reply was, "Well, I can talk the talk, it's time to go walk the walk." The simplistic thinking of youth, but telling nonetheless. Passing through that portal was a rite of passage, as it has been for so many others over the centuries. Seeking out an active battle front was another. Say what you will, but the experience of conflict has been one of those rites that men have engaged in, to be judged by, communally, since men first picked up a stone to defend their tribe.

So along came a war to make men free in Jugoslavia. I had gotten a 98 on the OCS test, one hungover morning on a drill weekend. My unit was very keen to send me, saying, "Jim, you're one of the few people here who actually gives a damn." But my ETS date was coming up fast as well, and in my thinking how could you be a good officer without having seen the real thing?

The conflict in Croatia and Bosnia was leading the news at the time and it was well known that foreign volunteers were flocking in, just as they had to Spain in 1933. The path was set. I would go do this and if I survived I would come back, reenlist, and then we could do all that OCS stuff. "They're killing women and children in the streets of an Olympic city and no one is doing anything about it. I've got skills, I might be useful," I recall telling a friend.

Problem was, I never came back. A few months turned into a few years, in and out of that place. Other places followed. Russia, Central Asia, the

Middle East, Latin America, and even a few hot spots stateside. I tumbled down different rabbit holes, stepped through a few different looking glasses, worked in a few different fields, but always came back for more. There were a lot of missteps, there was a lot of growing up.

Through it all, however, my experience and perceptions grew and matured. Conflict is really the one place where you can see the human animal in its full spectrum. All the window dressings get stripped away. There's the one end, way over there, of goodness, self-sacrifice, bravery under adversity. The higher virtues that Lincoln called, "The better angels of our nature." And then there's the other, way down that way, of selfishness, fear, hatred, depravity. The base drives that Freud termed "The Id." You see it all, you find your place in it. Which side of the spectrum are you going to fall on? You will find out very quickly.

Despite lots of temptation, lots of suffering, lots of anger and resentment, I still found myself on the good side. At the end of the day, you do the right thing, even if it leaves you in the lurch, which it so often does. That is where the character of your ancestors will lead you if you listen to them. Despite whatever their individual shortcomings, there is a theme of serving a higher cause that runs through their stories. That was certainly drilled into me by my WW2 father. "Think of others before you think of yourself," my Dad said more than once. It was something his entire generation lived up to.

It's not the path to fame, glory, and riches, but I'll take it. I was apparently born into it and it will just have to work for me, which I find it generally does.

www.ingramcontent.com/pod-product-compliance
Lightning Source LLC
LaVergne TN
LVHW020643100826
845148LV00012B/2316